THE TWELVE RAY

CW00922511

*A Guide to the Rays of Light
and the Spiritual Hierarchy*

NATALIE SIAN GLASSON

DERWEN PUBLISHING
PEMBROKE · DYFED

First published in Great Britain by Derwen Publishing 2010.

Derwen Publishing,
3 Bengal Villas,
Pembroke, Dyfed,
Wales, SA71 4BH

A CIP catalogue for this book is available
from the British Library.

ISBN 978-1-907084-09-6

Design and production by David Porteous Editions.
www.davidporteous.com

Printed and bound in the UK.

For the souls who are special to me,

Neal, Janice, Doreen and Clare,

Thank you.

My gratitude is extended to the Creator and all my friends on the inner planes who support my growth and the manifestation of this book.

The Twelve Rays of Light is given as a gift and tool of guidance from my truth and through my channel for all. It is my hope that through the information provided you will develop and ignite your own exploration of the twelve rays of light and the mighty soul of the Creator.

Cherish every moment of your journey through the rays and know that you are one with the Creator, which is the greatest realisation and truth of all.

CONTENTS

PART 3: BEYOND THE PLANETARY LEVEL

PART 1
THE PLANETARY SPIRITUAL HIERARCHY

CHAPTER 1

AN EXPLANATION OF THE SPIRITUAL HIERARCHY
AND OUR PLANETARY LEADERS

'Spiritual hierarchy' is a term often thrown into conversations of a spiritual nature to describe a group of light beings on the spiritual planes that are assisting the Earth in its evolution, acting as unseen forces. The word 'spiritual' can describe individuals or groups of people who have awoken to or realised the light of the Creator and are integrating the divine energies into their beings. A 'hierarchy' is defined as a group of individuals at different levels of ability and understanding, working in ranks or levels governed by a figure of authority.

Our Creator or God is the figure of authority who ultimately governs and oversees the Earth. Between the Earth and the Creator is a vast and intricate hierarchy of light beings who are all focusing their energy and light to the inhabitants of the Earth. We could call this the Earth's universe, as there are many other spiritual universes and hierarchies that extend from the different planets and stars in the open vastness of space. The Creator is a soul existing within a greater universe which is also sustained by a spiritual hierarchy.

The distance and levels through which a person on the Earth must progress to be reunited with the divine Creator are immeasurable, and continue once we reunite with the Creator. The Creator is our greater, wiser soul who embodies the entire universe, travelling on a spiritual journey with the inhabitants of the Earth and the Earth's spiritual hierarchy.

When we understand even a small amount about our journey we can comprehend the importance of our work on the Earth. Every action and advancement a soul achieves on the Earth assists the whole hierarchy within the Creator's universe to surge forward, raising the energy vibration of the Creator. It would seem that our work of growth and spiritual discovery is to aid and benefit the Creator; this is true, but we must remember that every soul on the Earth is a manifestation of the divine Creator, so in truth we are the Creator, and are working for our own spiritual growth and development.

The magnificent realm of the spiritual hierarchy exists on the inner planes as a consciousness invisible to the physical eyes of humans until they gain a significant understanding and awakening. We may imagine the universe as a continuum of layers, on each of which are thousands of light beings and souls working to develop their inner souls. Every soul on these levels has a mission to assist the souls below their level who are trying to grasp the ideas and enlightenment those above have already gained. This creates a chain assisting every soul in the universe to evolve and progress. Even though there are many souls existing at higher, more evolved levels than others, all are equal and loved by the Creator. They are just at different stages of awakening. If we take a single soul on the Earth, this physical soul may have some aspect of its being and light on every level of ascension within the hierarchy leading to the soul of the Creator, and each soul aspect is working to assist the souls at lower levels to evolve and understand the wisdom they have already gained. This may be hard to imagine, but it contributes to the realisation that all are connected and acting as one, eventually to become whole with the Creator. Even when this is achieved, the journey doesn't end but is continuous and eternal.

We can compare the spiritual hierarchy to a large pyramid structure as seen within a commercial company on Earth. We have the Chief Executive or Chairman of the company representing our Creator; there is a team of workers who have different roles, responsibilities, abilities and ranks within the company. Some workers have small responsibilities while others hold the company together, overseeing almost everything. It is the mission of the workers with only a small amount of responsibility to progress through the ranks to gain a higher salary and a greater influence within the company. The workers who are already near the top of the pyramid either retain their position, devoting their life to the company, or move on to a different company to offer their skills and understanding to others. These other companies could be compared to the different universes and spiritual hierarchies existing outside the Earth's universe.

As humans on the Earth we hold a small amount of responsibility, since we only have to master our beings and share our love with others. We must devote our time and focus to developing through the ranks. We will not receive a higher salary or recognition as in a physical company or business but we will embody the unconditional love of the Creator, gaining a greater unity with the Creator, which truthfully is the reason we came to the Earth. Earth is like a preparatory school which prepares us for the work we will carry out on the inner planes and during our ascension through the levels. This is the basic idea of the spiritual hierarchy. Of course there are exceptions: for instance, a soul who has already ascended and has broken away from the rebirth cycle of the Earth may choose to come back to the Earth in a physical body to assist in the awakening process of others. This doesn't mean they will have to achieve their ascension once more, as when they return to the inner planes and the spiritual hierarchy they will resume their previous position.

There are also many different paths, positions, roles and ways in which souls move through the spiritual hierarchy once they have left the Earth school. We will truly understand these when we ascend, breaking away from the Earth and mastering every aspect of our beings.

It is important as a physical being to develop an understanding of the spiritual hierarchy and to draw on the guidance, wisdom and light of the souls within this hierarchy and of our spiritual leaders. Having said this, we mustn't lose focus on our own realities on the Earth and our current mission of expansion and advancement, understanding and grasping the lessons of the Earth, moving through them to gain enlightenment. It is the Earth and physical reality that must remain our priority, drawing on the skills and tools given to us by evolved light beings on the inner planes to aid us in advancing spiritually.

The spiritual hierarchy can be broken down into layers or strata *(see diagram, page 14)*. As physical beings we exist within the lower levels of the first layer known as the *planetary* level, which is the closest to the Earth. Above the planetary level are the *solar* level, the *galactic* level, the *universal* level, the *multi-universal* level and the *cosmic* level. Each layer has many steps of growth and understanding to move through. There are souls or light beings who act as overseers and leaders of the souls in their care at each of the different levels of the spiritual hierarchy. The soul governing each layer has usually evolved through each level to acquire his or her title and role in the spiritual hierarchy and is continuing to grow using the role as a catalyst for spiritual advancement.

As humans we must first focus on the aspect of the spiritual hierarchy known as the planetary level, which is most accessible to us. The soul at the focal point of the planetary section is titled the *Planetary*

THE TWELVE RAYS OF LIGHT

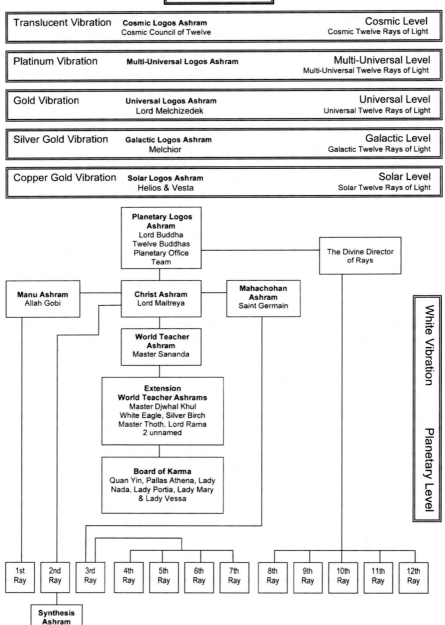

~ CREATOR ~

Translucent Vibration	**Cosmic Logos Ashram** Cosmic Council of Twelve	Cosmic Level Cosmic Twelve Rays of Light
Platinum Vibration	**Multi-Universal Logos Ashram**	Multi-Universal Level Multi-Universal Twelve Rays of Light
Gold Vibration	**Universal Logos Ashram** Lord Melchizedek	Universal Level Universal Twelve Rays of Light
Silver Gold Vibration	**Galactic Logos Ashram** Melchior	Galactic Level Galactic Twelve Rays of Light
Copper Gold Vibration	**Solar Logos Ashram** Helios & Vesta	Solar Level Solar Twelve Rays of Light

Planetary Logos Ashram
Lord Buddha
Twelve Buddhas
Planetary Office Team

The Divine Director of Rays

Manu Ashram
Allah Gobi

Christ Ashram
Lord Maitreya

Mahachohan Ashram
Saint Germain

World Teacher Ashram
Master Sananda

Extension World Teacher Ashrams
Master Djwhal Khul
White Eagle, Silver Birch
Master Thoth, Lord Rama
2 unnamed

Board of Karma
Quan Yin, Pallas Athena, Lady Nada, Lady Portia, Lady Mary & Lady Vessa

White Vibration

Planetary Level

1st Ray	2nd Ray	3rd Ray	4th Ray	5th Ray	6th Ray	7th Ray	8th Ray	9th Ray	10th Ray	11th Ray	12th Ray

Synthesis Ashram

Logos and named Lord Buddha. Lord Buddha is the president of the Earth; he oversees every human, animal, tree, plant and mineral on the Earth as well as all the many light beings who work as spiritual guides for each soul in physical manifestation and all the light beings who work with the Earth and Mother Earth. Lord Buddha has a deep connection with Mother Earth; they both unite with the planet and souls incarnated on the Earth. The sacred Goddess Mother Earth inhabits all aspects of physical matter, nature and physical bodies existing on her body labelled Earth; she is akin to a vast spirit or guardian at the core of the planet, integrated with everything. Lord Buddha's energy encapsulates the Earth from the inner planes; he oversees and exists as the spiritual energies and vibrations of the Earth. Every action, thought and energy he produces and emanates affects and influences the energy of the Earth.

People on the Earth have free will. Lord Buddha has to watch while the Earth and its inhabitants do as they please; he cannot assist them in any way unless they first ask for his aid. Lord Buddha instead reinforces his own spiritual awareness, understanding and love, placing it within and around the Earth, so that those who wish to evolve or connect with the Creator and the planetary spiritual hierarchy can access his energy for their own spiritual growth.

Lord Buddha works with many light workers on the Earth who are open and receptive to his thoughts and light, but he also sends waves of energy to raise the consciousness of the planet and awaken people to the light of the Creator. Each time a wave of energy descends from the Planetary Logos Ashram a few more people are inspired to seek the truth, and Mother Earth is healed and cleansed of the pain caused to her body by humanity. We must allow ourselves to be open to this energy surge as it comes forth from the highest energy being within our planetary level to assist us in accelerating our development. Lord Buddha is the bridge of light between the Earth and energy levels of the Creator's universe.

The position and role of every Master governing the higher layers of the hierarchy are similar to Lord Buddha's as Planetary Logos, but the responsibilities of the Solar Logos are greater than the Planetary Logos but less than the Galactic Logos, with the Universal Logos and the Multi-Universal Logos dominating the higher aspects of the Creator's universe overseen by the Cosmic Logos.

Lord Buddha is not alone in his work and mission. Many Masters and light beings exist within the numerous levels of the planetary section, assisting, supporting and integrating Lord Buddha's white vibration of light, which holds the consciousness of the planetary level. There is a team of pre-selected male and female Masters working within the ashram or sacred space of the Planetary Logos. Known as the Planetary Team, they assist with the general running of the ashram, greeting students and supporting Lord Buddha's Mission. The Divine Director of Rays extends from the Planetary Team; this Master oversees the higher rays eight to twelve of light, as well as generally supervising all twelve rays of light on Lord Buddha's behalf.

Lord Maitreya works closely with Lord Buddha, assisting the Earth in its spiritual evolution. Lord Maitreya holds the position of the Christ; he oversees the Christ Consciousness and the integration of the Creator's love with the souls on the Earth. In truth, Lord Maitreya not only embodies and radiates the Christ Consciousness energy, but is the Christ. The Christ Consciousness is of a golden colour and is the loving energy of the Creator which can be accessed by physical beings without harming them or being too powerful for the level at which they vibrate. When souls become integrated and understand the Christ Consciousness, having the ability to embody and anchor it into their life, then they will be able to ascend to a new level of consciousness, accepting themselves as a manifestation of the Creator and acting as a manifestation of the Creator on the Earth. This is not in any egotistical sense, but by using the loving energy of the Creator and embodying it in mind, body, emotions, soul and actions, one can become integrated. Lord Maitreya acts as a spiritual teacher of the Christ Consciousness to aid the spiritual growth of humankind on the Earth as well as the light beings that assist humankind and exist within the planetary level. It is Lord Maitreya's duty to pour the loving energy of the Christ into all twelve rays of light at a planetary level, the twelfth ray being the Christ Consciousness energy, demonstrating the immense power of, and necessity for, love.

In the planetary section or level we have twelve rays of light available to us for our use; each ray is an expression of the Creator's love and holds different qualities to assist humans in their development and unification with the Creator's soul. Becoming integrated with these rays and the Christ consciousness is the mission of physical beings on the Earth to aid discovery of the Creator's soul.

Lord Maitreya forms a trinity with the Manu and the Mahachohan, the 'heads of department' who oversee the rays, their Chohans or governors of each ray, and the Masters. The Manu is the title of the overseer of the first ray of light currently known as Allah Gobi. Lord Maitreya oversees the second ray of light, and the Mahachohan Saint Germain oversees the rays that extend from the third ray of light.

These three hold a huge responsibility for the students incarnating on the Earth; they act as spiritual mentors, assist in the awakening and growth of the world, and support the work of Lord Buddha. Their roles are greatly significant for our planet and our advancement as they aid and guide us in ways we cannot comprehend. Through their roles and positions as leaders and devotees of the Earth they are learning to advance their own spiritual development. They are assisting us at a planetary level, but in terms of their spiritual education they may be enrolled at a universal or cosmic level of the spiritual hierarchy. It is this trinity of Masters that we can invoke to assist and support our spiritual work on the Earth because it is their mission to be open to the invocations and calls of any being on the Earth.

The trinity of Masters and Lord Buddha are not alone in their efforts and leadership of the Earth; there are many teams and realms of light beings working behind the scenes on their and our behalf. For each ray of light a Chohan is appointed to govern the ray, its development and work on the inner planes and on the Earth. Assisting each Chohan are many Ascended Masters, Goddesses, Archangels, Angels, Elementals and light beings. While the Chohans or governors of the rays may devote their focus to a particular ray, they have integrated with all twelve rays of light and are working to unite the rays. This means that although a Chohan may be known for working on one ray, his or her allegiance also remains with several other rays of light. All rays are united as one and all Chohans or governors of the rays are united as one; they have just chosen for now to devote their energy to a particular ray that resonates with their current mission or process of growth.

There are, of course, many other Masters and groups assisting the development of the planet. Master Sananda is working to educate the Earth spiritually, but it is Lord Buddha, together with the trinity, and the twelve rays of light with their Chohans and teams, that are at the focal point of the Earth's growth, and can be invoked or worked with to assist development.

It is important for us to learn from these beings, integrating and understanding the energy and practices they present us with, before we connect with the Masters and light beings from the higher levels or sections of Earth's spiritual hierarchy. These planetary Masters, the twelve rays of light and their assistants, are here for us now. They offer wisdom, light and their love to whomsoever invokes their support. It is important to create special bonds with these prominent Masters as it is they who will oversee our route of ascension through the planetary spiritual hierarchy after we overcome the challenges and lessons of the Earth.

It is necessary for us to understand that we have come to the Earth to experience the planetary level and its Masters in a physical body. When we have achieved the goals of our souls, discarding our physical vehicles and ascending into the spiritual world, we will then experience and integrate the planetary level once more within a light body, but with an enhanced level of consciousness. A light body is a sacred grid-work of light that anchors into our physical body with spiritual development to aid ascension. It houses our soul when we evolve from our physical existence and when we travel to ashrams on the inner planes during our sleep states. There are many different aspects of our light body that we can anchor from each level of the spiritual hierarchy to gain illumination and integration with the Creator's energy and universe.

It is wonderful that we have such amazing and radiant light beings working with us and the Earth; most of these light beings have achieved ascension from the Earth, and therefore hold an accurate understanding of the journey that lies ahead for us.

CHAPTER 2

ASCENDING MASTERS

An Ascended Master is an individual from the energy or inner planes of the spiritual world who has incarnated onto the Earth several times in different embodiments to gain enlightenment and mastery in a physical body. The individual creates and attracts many lessons, challenges and experiences in its lifetime on the Earth to enhance its spiritual awareness, luminosity and connection with the Creator and inner soul. The lessons can be tough, depending on the soul's goals and the plans the soul created before the embodiment, but every aspect of the life is aimed at the growth of the spiritual being and mastery of the physical body. Once the individual has discovered how to lovingly control the emotions, thoughts, personality and actions of the physical aspect, as well as gaining unity with the Creator at a planetary level, he or she is allowed to move on to the next stage of their spiritual growth.

This doesn't necessarily mean the individual will break away from the Earth and the rebirth system of the planet to take a position or role in the spiritual hierarchy. Some individuals may wish to continue living in their physical body to use their newly appointed mastery and understanding to assist other humans in awakening and focusing their energy. They may even choose to gain integration with the higher levels of the Creator's universe while on the Earth. Others choose to return to the Earth in a new body to help raise the energy vibration of the Earth, or prefer to follow a path in the spiritual planes, allowing them to assist in the awakening of humanity. Many of the Ascended Masters working with the twelve rays of light and the planetary level have a passion for assisting humans in their spiritual education. There are many routes for individuals or souls who have mastered their physical being to take in order to move closer to the mighty soul of the Creator.

Nearly every soul who focuses on the light of the Creator in the higher planetary layers holds an Ascended Master consciousness. We are mostly aware of the Ascended Masters who have taken up positions as leaders within the spiritual hierarchy to lovingly care and encourage the spiritual growth of the planet Earth and its inhabitants, but there are many more Ascended Masters who act as unseen forces within the universe. Not all Ascended Masters have evolved from the Earth; some have gained their spiritual education and mastery from the many schools - planets and stars within and outside our universe. At this current time, the Earth is a tool assisting many students in overcoming their challenges and anchoring their soul and *monad*, or soul group, into their physical bodies. Nearly every person on the Earth exists here because they are trying to gain spiritual and physical mastery; the other small percentages of incarnate souls are helping their soul extensions, or the entire civilisation, to rise in consciousness.

Each of us has a path of light before us that will lead us to embodying our soul, the energy of the Creator and an advanced limitless awareness. This path of light continues once we leave the Earth and step into the spiritual world and universe. We may have free will on the Earth, but our souls have created goals to be overcome; every situation in our lives is to enhance spiritual growth. Once we accept this we understand not to ignore problems or situations in our lives, as we will only have to come back to the Earth again to resolve them. Each lesson is either created by our minds, souls, guides or the Creator. The mind has the power to manifest anything we desire on the Earth - and sometimes creates negative situations if it is not programmed. These are not necessarily lessons sent from or planned by the soul for growth, but are warnings that mastery of the mind must be obtained.

Every person on the Earth is an Ascended Master, they are just at different stages of realisation; they have either not discovered this for themselves, or are evolving towards attaining their Ascended Master consciousness, or are a fully formed Ascended Master. This makes us appreciate that any person we meet on the streets could be a realised Ascended Master and that we must honour the divine within every person who crosses our path. To be clear, we could say all beings are ascending masters because even the souls who have broken away from the rebirth cycle of the Earth and have been given the title of an Ascended Master are continuing to ascend through the ranks of the spiritual planes. The Archangels and Angels, although they may not have walked physically on the Earth, are progressing and growing through their work with us on the Earth. Consequently they are ascending.

The Ascended Masters who exist on the spiritual planes make themselves available to assist us on the Earth; their key focus is the wellbeing and growth of the Earth and its inhabitants. They have allowed it to become their mission to assist us on the Earth because of their love for every soul extension of the Creator. They understand they are manifestations of the Creator, and in order to become united with the Creator they must assist the other soul extensions of the Creator in evolving as well. There isn't a gap between the souls embodied on the Earth and the Ascended Masters; they haven't stepped away from us, accelerating forth to be united with the Creator. The Ascended Masters are constantly supporting us. They throw us ropes and lifelines persistently, to allow us to step onto our spiritual paths and master our beings. They are akin to mothers and fathers helping their children to awaken to the great and vast world around them. They teach the children to grow, offering them tools and encouragement to achieve their goals. We must honour the Ascended Masters for helping us, but we must remember they are just like us; they simply mastered their beings before us.

The titles given to the Masters within the spiritual hierarchy are simply labels portraying their responsibilities; these titles are not important but help us to understand their roles further. Their title doesn't signify that they are better or more valuable than we are; it simply honours the spiritual growth they have achieved. Many channels and light workers give a variety of labels or titles to our planetary leaders and a diversity of Masters as our leaders; this is due to their different backgrounds and education, as well as the great volume of Masters wishing to assist us. It is important for us to focus on connecting and receiving energy in whichever way is appropriate for us, rather than allowing their labels to confuse us. We are all loved equally by the Creator and must love ourselves as equals.

Ascended Masters are both male and female, originating from many different spiritual backgrounds and homes within the universe and a variety of cultures and realities on the Earth. The life they led while on the Earth can determine the focus of their energy in the spiritual world. Masters who spend their lifetimes on the Earth healing others may focus their energies with a healing ray, team or group in the spiritual world; they may even continue to focus on developing their healing abilities, enrolling themselves in a school for spiritual advancement in or beyond our universe. Masters may choose to develop the healing skills of souls incarnate on the Earth from their position on the spiritual planes and dimensions. The work the Masters complete and achieve on the Earth can mould their future in the spiritual world and hierarchy. This implies that we must value and honour every aspect of our lives and the abilities of our beings, respecting the divine within us to discover the true purposes of our existence on the Earth, which may awaken and guide us to the possible purposes, roles or positions we could obtain in the spiritual planes when we evolve from the Earth.

Understanding the past lifetimes of Ascended Masters allows us only to glimpse a small percentage of their true and whole beings, but can inspire us to reach beyond the limitations we have created for our lives on the Earth. We can see the attainments that can be achieved when focus is applied, but we mustn't allow this understanding to lead us onto an incorrect path for our souls. As ascending masters, we must be true to ourselves, allowing our souls to guide us to achieve the necessary realisations to assist us in becoming Masters. It is valuable to understand that although there are many Ascended Masters whose past lifetimes are famous and renowned for the development of our civilisation, equally there are thousands who appeared to have lived average lives while on the Earth, but the truth is they were living and working within their bodies. Their minds were focused on their souls and their connection with the Creator as they enjoyed the simple things in life or devoted their energy to care for and heal others in their own special way. These Ascended Masters have assisted in the rise of Mother Earth's energy vibration and now work in the spiritual world as invisible, or rather unknown forces to us. Their work is equally as important as that of the Ascended Masters that are currently well-known by light workers on the Earth.

There is a tremendous amount of love, light and high vibrational energy descending from the spiritual hierarchy and the Ascended Masters. Many Masters are now making themselves known to humanity, while others are increasing the volume of light entering into the Earth. This is all with the purpose of accelerating the spiritual growth of every soul. The Ascended Masters, whether they work on a planetary or universal level, wish to act as our mentors, guides and spiritual teachers; who better to guide us than the souls who have already achieved what we are striving for? It is their existence in the spiritual hierarchy, their roles and the rays of light they use to assist the Earth and humanity, that are most inspiring for us on the Earth. Understanding the light and energy they work with will help us to gain a deeper association with the Masters, building a bridge of light between the Earth and the spiritual hierarchy.

By listing and describing the roles of our spiritual leaders or Ascended Masters, I wish to assist in anchoring the light, love and wisdom of these great beings into the Earth and within the hearts of many. I have given only a small explanation of their past lives as I believe these can be easily researched using physical tools; it is the Ascended Masters' positions on the inner planes and the rays of light they work with that are not so readily available or accessible, causing confusion to many. I have gathered the wisdom and roles of some of the Ascended Masters and our focal spiritual leaders through my channelling ability, and by direct communication, to assist light workers in gaining more clarity when connecting with these divine spiritual teachers.

Let us open our hearts to the Ascended Masters from all backgrounds and walks of life, allowing them to lead us forth with their bright blazing beacons of the Creator's light. Let us allow them to assist us in accepting ourselves as ascending masters to become fully realised Ascended Masters on the Earth, emanating our Ascended Master consciousness to raise the energy vibration of humanity and the entire spiritual hierarchy.

CHAPTER 3

RECONNECTING WITH THE ASCENDING MASTERS AND OUR SPIRITUAL LEADERS

We all can recognise the feeling of resonance or connection with an Ascended Master or light being when we read about them or hear someone talk about them. This sensation of familiarity or reflex attraction can be a symbol of the bonds that have already been made in past lifetimes, or can lead us to believe a Master we were previously unaware of is assisting us. It is important to follow our intuition or gut feelings on these occasions; especially after reading about individual Ascended Masters, doubt may creep in from the ego, but we must hold faith in our initial feelings of familiarity as it is these that stem from the soul. All of us on the Earth have Ascended Masters guiding us. They may exist within our personal community of guides, helping us with every step of our lives, or they may oversee our path and progress, assisting when greater inspiration or aid is needed. Lord Buddha, for example, is an Ascended Master guide to every soul on the Earth.

When we make a connection with an Ascended Master, it is not a new friendship that is formed, but rather recognition of the souls who are assisting us. With practice and focus we can expand our realisation of this connection to receive greater wisdom and guidance from the Masters. A connection can also be defined as absorbing or anchoring energy into our physical bodies and souls from another light being. In truth, when we make a connection with a Master, we experience their energy and awaken to their presence around us, uniting with an aspect of the Creator.

Sometimes we are attracted to an Ascended Master because of the skills or teachings they can assist us in gaining. Other times it is their loving soul or energy drawing us to work with them. It is beneficial to understand the reasons we feel a resonance with a certain Master so we can learn to allow them and ourselves to move on, once we have grasped the lessons or skills they wish to bestow on us. Some Ascended Masters will stay by our sides for the whole of our lives on the Earth acting as personal guides, while others will make contact at pinnacle points in our spiritual journeys. When we understand that every soul on the Earth and in the spiritual hierarchy is interconnected, we realise we have a connection with every Ascended Master; it's just that there are some Masters with whom we have worked frequently in the past and so a deeper relationship has formed.

To reconnect with the Ascended Masters and to expand our realisation is easy. It doesn't have to be complicated or taxing because the Creator works in the simplest of ways. It is the Creator's wish to be united with all the soul extensions on the Earth, as all are a part of the Creator's mighty soul. The Creator encourages us with every thought in the mighty mind and every particle of love in the mighty heart; it is the ego and fear created by the human mind that cause confusion and difficulties. If every person were to spend every part of their day with every aspect of their being connected to the Creator, then all obstacles would be removed and life would flow with harmony and love for all. There are exceptions within this notion, as the soul can sometimes create a negative situation to allow a tremendous growth process to be overcome, but it would be far easier for us to overcome these challenges with the love of the Creator manifested in our hearts.

Embracing the truth of the Creator, we can comprehend that we only need simple practices with unbreakable focus and faith to create miracles in our lives and to evolve into an accomplished Master of our physical aspect. There are so many practices, meditations, invocations and directions given to light workers on the Earth for spiritual enhancement that it can become overwhelming. We can sometimes lose our focus on the truth and even our mission.

One of our missions is to connect with the Creator through the Ascended Masters, Angels, Archangels and light beings the Creator sends to guide us. The other mission is to accept and integrate our souls and physical aspects with the twelve rays of light. The energy of the Creator holds a magnitude of power and could be too intense for the physical shell to embody entirely on the Earth, so it is filtered down through the levels of the spiritual hierarchy until it vibrates at an appropriate energetic rate that will not burn up the physical body. While we must create a direct connection with the Creator, we must realise that linking with aspects of the Creator such as the Ascended Masters and the rays of light enables us to discover and explore the

25

consciousness and qualities of the Creator.

Everything in this world is comprised of energy. The Creator is a manifestation of energy, so it seems appropriate that to accelerate our spiritual growth we must focus on feeling the energy of the Ascended Masters and light beings in and around our beings, using the power of our minds and voices to invoke these high vibrational energies. To ascend, to develop our spiritual beings, we must absorb more of the loving positive light energy into our bodies, focusing our minds on this throughout the day.

Connection Exercise
The simplest way of connecting with an Ascended Master, spiritual leader or the Creator is by sitting peacefully, focusing on your breathing to create a meditative state of mind and being. Allow your breathing to deepen and your body to relax; counting to ten or twenty and stating each number on each breath may assist you in focusing your mind. If you are accustomed to meditating then follow your own practice of gaining a relaxed and receptive state of being. Then you may invoke Archangel Michael, the great powerful protector of humankind against negativity, and distributor of the will of the Creator.

It is a wise idea to decide who you wish to communicate with before you begin the meditation, as the Master will hear your thoughts and prepare to make a connection with you.

Ask either in your mind or aloud for Archangel Michael to oversee your meditation and to surround you in a large bubble of blue and silver light which acts as a shield resting around the edge of your aura. This shield of blue and silver light is impenetrable to anything that is not of light or love consciousness.

In your meditative state of being, invoke the Master you wish to communicate with by repeating their name for a few minutes, asking them to surround you in their positive loving soul energy, while also channelling their energy into your being through your crown chakra at the top of your head. Let this request flow naturally from your being. You cannot make a mistake. Within this book invocations are very rarely given as we each have the ability to create our own invocations from our hearts, making them personal and powerful.

The energy of the Master will begin to surge through you, entering in through your crown chakra at the top of your head, down your column of chakra systems: the third eye, throat, heart, solar plexus, sacral and root chakras.

As the energy flows into your crown chakra, it will also activate your soul star chakra, which is approximately six inches above your head. The soul star chakra is connected with the earth star chakra approximately six to twelve inches below the feet; it causes an imbalance in your energy if one is activated without the other. It is important when invoking the energy of a Master to allow the light to flow down your chakra column and into the core of Mother Earth. This way, both chakras remain balanced and activated. It is crucial always to share any energy you receive or absorb from the spiritual planes with Mother Earth, as she is following her own spiritual growth process and needs a wealth of healing and light rays of a high vibration anchored into the core of her body.

Sit peacefully and enjoy the sensations of the energy surging through your body. Focus on your breathing and imagine that with every breath you inhale, you are absorbing into your body the light the Master has filled your aura with. When you physically absorb light into your body through your breath, you anchor the light deeper into your physical form.

This is the main purpose of this meditation: to teach us to understand and feel the energies of the Masters around us. We can continuously ask the Masters to enhance the strength and intensity of the light and energy we receive until we can fully experience its presence.

We can practise this simple meditation of sitting and breathing in the light with any Master and ray of light, as it creates a connection and focuses the mind on the light entering into the body. From this state of absorption, connection and illumination, we can accomplish many things, accessing greater spiritual development. It is not the process that is beneficial but the experience gained through simple meditations while invoking and absorbing light. This meditation should increase your faith in the presence of the Ascended Masters in your life, as you will be able to feel the vibrations and sensations of their energy around and running through your body. You will also accept their consciousness or wisdom into your aura, enlightening you further.

The important key when wishing to communicate with the Masters is to talk to them. This can be out loud or in your mind. Tell them you wish to connect and communicate with them, inform them that you wish to evolve spiritually with the ability to understand their wisdom.

You can talk to them about any problems in your life, asking them to assist and support you. Talking openly to the Ascended Masters appears to be such a simple idea, but it opens your energy systems and allows the Masters to intervene in your life, removing all blockages that may have been created by fear of communicating.

If you remain in an open, relaxed and meditative state of being while you talk to them and then rest silently, with practice you will begin to gain insights: images, words or ideas will enter into your mind. It is essential to remain aware and to hold faith in your own abilities. Trust what you are given. If you feel that it is just in your imagination, then indulge it, as this will build energy and remove blockages to allow the true communication to flow into your mind. It may help to write down any words or images you receive to study later or to increase the flow of energy entering into your mind. Remember, as your faith and confidence grow, so your ability to communicate will blossom.

If this process works for you, then you can use it to gain a volume of information from the Masters you wish to communicate with. It is important for us to find our own ways of connecting and communicating with them, allowing the creative juices to flow from our souls while following our natural instincts. When we use specific prayers and invocations these can sometimes hinder our own inner wisdom, power and natural ways from blossoming from within our beings, but when we invoke the energy of the rays or Masters, we can be sure of their presence around us, using their energy as a springboard for our further growth. When we have gained a certain amount of wisdom about the spiritual hierarchy and the rays it becomes easy and simple for us to create our own invocations that are personal to our growth. We all know how to connect and communicate with the Ascended Masters, we just haven't remembered it yet or realised the wisdom existing within our souls.

While experiencing the energy of an Ascended Master and comparing it with your connection experiences with other Masters, you may realise that each has his or her own energy signature, announced by a familiar sensation on any part of your body. Recognising the energy signature of each Ascended Master can help you to distinguish, with assurance, which one is drawing close to you or assisting you in your daily life.

Feeling the energy of a Master running through your body when invoked will give you the trust, faith and confidence you need to begin communicating with that Master. Imagining the light of the Creator and the Master of your choice entering into your being through your crown chakra can begin the process of gaining clear communication from the Master through a channel.

A channel is like an invisible tube built into your crown chakra that extends into the heavens; the channel is built from light and allows light, energy and wisdom to enter into the human mind. You can ask the Ascended Masters and the Creator to begin to build your channel to enhance your communicative skills. Imagining light entering your crown chakra will activate the building work of a channel or communication tube. I must warn that the building of a channel and even the absorbing of light can cause discomfort, especially headaches, due to blockages being released and the volume of energy entering your body to support the work of the Masters. If this occurs, ask the Masters to ease your discomfort and take time to relax and breathe deeply. Don't give up; believing that something negative is occurring will only cause greater distress. If you have felt the energy of the Masters and become accustomed to receiving it, then you must hold faith that their work is for your greater spiritual growth process.

To increase our abilities to connect with the Masters, we need to practise using our thoughts to ask the Master of our choice to increase the amount of light in our bodies. A human body may be compared to a crystal, which needs energy anchored into its being in order to be programmed to work and be activated; otherwise its energy can become stale. It is the same for the physical body and aura. When we do not absorb light into our bodies or ask for our light quotients to be increased, we are not activating the energy within our beings, and so the chakra systems slow down and can become blocked, leaving the physical body to stagnate. This is when illness can form. When light runs continuously into the physical body, all blockages are reduced and the general health of the body is enhanced, because the soul and chakra systems are receiving the energy they need to function.

It is important not only to imagine and breathe light into our bodies, but to ask the Masters of our choice to increase or double the amount of light within our bodies and every aspect of our beings. When we ask, we always receive divine intervention. By asking frequently throughout the day we will multiply the light existing and running through our bodies. When the Masters examine humans on the Earth, they view our growth process by establishing the amount of light within the physical body and aura. Obtaining light means that we hold a greater awareness; light and energy are the keys to ascension as they have huge transformational effects on the body and are the essence of our souls. Archangel Metatron and Master Vywamus are Cosmic Masters who are particularly skilled in increasing our light quotients and energy vibrations to higher levels than they currently vibrate at.

An example of requesting additional light could be:

'I invoke Archangel Metatron to increase or double the amount of light within every aspect of my being, ensuring I receive the perfect amount and vibration of energy for my body and growth.'

We can request this every hour of our day or more if we wish, but we must try to understand our light limits, establishing the amount of light that is safe for the body and isn't overwhelming. If you feel unwell or uncomfortable with the amount of light energy entering your body, don't stop the flow completely, but ask for the energy to be toned down a fraction. You should feel a tingling sensation as the light channels into your crown chakra, but it shouldn't be overpowering. You can then forget about it until you wish to request again. A wonderful request and experience is to invoke Lord Maitreya to increase and intensify the body of love within your being.

Visiting the inner planes, the sacred ashrams or the Masters in their light bodies seems like a wonderful dream, but it is one that can be accomplished and offers great support to the spiritual journey of a human on the Earth, aiding and developing connections and communication with the Masters. We can visit the inner planes during our sleep states on the Earth. When we sleep we allow our bodies to rest and rejuvenate; it is also important to allow our souls and light bodies to do the same. We can ask to be taken to any Ascended Master's ashram within the spiritual hierarchy as long as we ask our personal Angels to support us and ensure our safe return to our bodies on the Earth.

Some of you may already have places you visit on the inner planes for learning and lectures, or you may not be aware of the journey your soul already makes each night, but it doesn't do any harm to ask to be taken to a certain place or Master as it ensures you continue to grow and learn even when your body is asleep. When describing the Ascended Masters, I will mention which you can visit on the spiritual planes, and the rays on which you may find them, but most are accessible.

Everything you learn and gain when you visit the ashrams of the Masters and the rays of light will be retained in your aura and will filter into your mind when you are awake on the Earth and ready to receive it. To achieve and experience this, simply ask your personal Angels before you fall asleep at night to take you to the place of your choice and to ensure your safety at all times. Ask to wake up in the morning remembering your journey, with a feeling of vitality and radiant health. It is acceptable to visit different places each night, while it is also agreeable to ask your soul to journey to wherever it wishes, to gain the wisdom, light and healing it needs to accelerate your spiritual growth on the Earth. By practising this device for growth and connection, you will integrate and embody greater wisdom, light and love into your physical body and reality.

It is wonderful and rewarding to devote oneself to the Creator and grasp the support, love and guidance the Masters offer us on the Earth, as they are here to assist us in mastering our beings, but we must learn not to give our power away to them. Equally, the Ascended Masters must also learn not to give their power away to us when helping us on the Earth. It is their mission to share their wisdom, love and soul light with us, but they also have to focus on their own roles and growth, ensuring they do not become so involved in our lives that we no longer make decisions for ourselves. We need to learn to accept the assistance and energy of the Ascended Masters and the Creator, while not allowing ourselves to withdraw from forming our own opinions and following the guidance of our souls.

The Ascended Masters are our teachers, but it is our souls that are the driving force of our lives and journeys on the Earth. To ensure we retain our own inner power, we can accept and understand the guidance given to us from the Masters, and can then integrate this with the guidance given to us by physical light beings on the Earth. With the insights we gain, we must consult our inner souls, asking whether this information is true and acceptable for our own growth processes.

Following our own intuition and consulting the inner soul is a form of self-mastery. On the Earth we give our power away without realising because we are not constantly in contact with our soul light/Creator presence and inner wisdom. People make decisions for us that affect our lives all the time. They tell us information and we accept it as the truth, when we should allow our soul light to shine brightly, consulting it on every aspect of our lives because it is our true selves, an aspect of the Creator within us. Then we can lovingly agree or lovingly disagree: we have the power to achieve this loving state, of being a Master of every aspect of our lives. There is a fine line between controlling our lives with the ego and accepting the wisdom of our souls. It is our responsibility to allow our soul light to become a greater influence in our lives. We must also remember we are equal in the eyes of the Creator to the Ascended Masters and are ascending masters ourselves.

It is important for us to remain open-minded and receptive to the wisdom of the Ascended Masters and other light workers on the Earth because we can discover new perspectives from each other. Much information has been shared through many mediums and channels over the years. This information has created a well of knowledge from which we can draw to heighten our spiritual growth, but we must remember that the spiritual hierarchy, the Earth and the awareness of souls in the universe is constantly changing. It is our responsibility to access information through our souls and the Ascended Masters that is appropriate to the modern day on the Earth. This allows us to be open to the wisdom of new light channels, or even the reincarnation of Ascended Masters onto the Earth with new teachings.

Will we have the courage to accept their energy and information if it is different to what we are accustomed to hearing? We will if we are connected to our souls because we will be able to distinguish the truth from the ego of the human mind. When we expand our minds beyond our current state of awareness, we are able to gain new wisdom that applies to the Earth now. We are in such a unique position of accelerated growth as a civilisation that we must learn to love one another and to follow the book of truth within our souls, encapsulated by our physical bodies, while allowing the Ascended Masters to inspire the truth from within us.

It is for this reason that you may not find all the answers you are looking for in this book: it is up to you to search within your soul to gain the answers you seek, but I hope that knowing about the amazing Ascended Masters and rays of light that are available to work with will give you a helpful start on your process of growth, and most importantly, help you reconnect with these Masters to experience the full intensity of their energy and the love they hold for all.

Let us now embark on gaining a greater understanding of the Ascended Masters and our spiritual leaders, so we may use this knowledge to increase our bond and realisation of them and the spiritual hierarchy that watch over our lives and guide us to live in unity with the Creator.

CHAPTER 4
PLANETARY LOGOS LORD BUDDHA

Lord Buddha is the Earth's Planetary Logos; he is the highest being in the spiritual government on a planetary level. In a sense Buddha is the president or world leader in the spiritual planes. The word *Buddha* means one who has awoken to enlightenment, while the word *Logos* is a title used to describe the source of world order or one who holds and understands the Creator's will. By understanding the simple meaning of Lord Buddha's title we are able to gain an understanding of his mission on our behalf for the Earth.

Lord Buddha is an Ascended Master who has experienced numerous lifetimes on the Earth. He has evolved from a physical life when he was known as Siddhartha Gautama. He gained enlightenment, an insight into the nature of life and spiritual discipline on the Earth through his physical experiences and exploration of his heart and mind. The accelerated growth of Siddhartha Gautama in his lifetime on the Earth allowed him to become known as Buddha. After evolving to such a high energy vibration and spiritual awareness on the Earth, Buddha then stepped into the spiritual hierarchy on the inner planes and began his spiritual development again on a new energy vibration with a new level of consciousness. In a sense it would have been similar to starting at the beginning of a higher advanced school of learning. He was at the foot of the spiritual hierarchy on the inner planes, ready to evolve through the many roles and paths that the spiritual hierarchy has to offer to accelerate his spiritual growth further. Buddha as an Ascended Master became known as Lord Buddha. His lifetime on the Earth inspired the tradition and teachings of Buddhism.

Lord Buddha enrolled on a path of education on the inner planes to become a Logos or overseer; this is a disciplined tuition that allowed his embodiment of the Planetary Logos position. Lord Buddha graciously replaced the previous Planetary Logos Sanat Kumara in 1994, after overshadowing his work for some time. This allowed Sanat

Kumara to continue with his own spiritual evolution. In his training to become Planetary Logos, Lord Buddha acted as a teacher within the second ray of light and studied in the Christ Ashram as well as connecting with the higher levels of the Creator's universe to gain a wider view of the will of the Creator. It is because of his roles in the past that he holds a deep connection with the second ray of light of love and wisdom and the golden energy of the Christ Consciousness; these energies are evident in Lord Buddha's soul energy. Lord Buddha has evolved through many initiations and growth processes that are beyond our current understanding, to act as spiritual leader and overseer of the Earth on a planetary level.

Lord Buddha oversees every single soul and their mission on the Earth as if he is caring for a child or a loved one. He oversees our growth and development as well as ensuring that the vibration of the Earth rises at a balanced speed. Loving us unconditionally, he understands that we are part of his being and soul; we are connected in union with Lord Buddha and Mother Earth. Mother Earth's energy will always remain with the Earth even as it evolves; she is its essence, while Lord Buddha oversees the Earth and its inhabitants until he completes his mission and growth. In truth, we as humans are an important part of a trinity between Lord Buddha and Mother Earth. We must accept our precious place on the Earth and use our time to grow spiritually, thus assisting Mother Earth and Lord Buddha in ascending in energy vibration.

Lord Buddha has not only devoted himself completely to the Creator, understanding himself to be a manifestation of the Creator's energy, but he has enrolled himself as a protector and adviser of every constituent of the Creator's mighty soul who is in existence on the Earth and in the spiritual hierarchy at a planetary level. His responsibilities are enormous and yet he still views every aspect of the Earth as a vital part of his soul and energy. As physical beings on the Earth, we can understand the difficulty of spiritual progression in a physical reality. Imagine if we had not only to focus on our own growth but the growth and experiences of every person existing on the Earth as well as the animal, mineral and plant kingdoms! This is the role of Lord Buddha from his ashram in the spiritual planes; he is our support system and our link to the energy of the Creator.

Lord Buddha doesn't complete his mission alone as he has twelve evolved and enlightened Buddhas who work closely with him to aid the Earth. There is also a team of Masters working within the Planetary Logos Ashram to assist Lord Buddha. He receives support from the light beings at a planetary level and the great Cosmic Masters of the universe who are in the spiritual chain above him. Lord Buddha's deep connection with the Creator and the wisdom of his soul and higher aspects also guide him in his important role for us on the Earth.

As spiritual leader of our planet Lord Buddha is available to work with us to advance our spiritual evolution. We can call on his energy, light and wisdom to guide us in our lives. To invoke Lord Buddha's energy to assist us, we must simply call out his name with love in our hearts or repeat the mantra, 'I am Buddha,' which will connect us with his divine energies. The energy radiating from Lord Buddha's soul is of a white colour, as the consciousness and teachings of the planetary level are held within this colour of energy, but in truth he embodies and oversees all twelve rays of light and the Christ consciousness. It can depend on many circumstances as to which energy is most prominent in Lord Buddha's energy field at various periods and times when we invoke his energy. It could be our need for certain energies, or his focus that allows us to connect with the different light rays within his soul light.

When we invoke Lord Buddha it is important to ask him not only to surround our beings in his energy, but to channel his white pure light into our beings, allowing the light to travel in through our crown chakra, down our chakra column and into the Earth. This is a request that we can ask of all the Ascended Masters and the Creator, as it ensures we receive the full benefits of their energy and anchors their soul light into our beings, aiding us to increase the amount of light within our bodies. With practice this will become a natural habit when invoking light beings to assist us.

Lord Buddha's energy and light will not only elevate the amount of light in our bodies, but also his energy holds a vast wealth of wisdom and enlightenment as well as healing qualities and inspirational thought forms. Lord Buddha is dedicated to his work: he is such a joyous being, filled with so much love of the purest form, that when we invoke his energy he can fill our lives with great happiness, while also protecting and overseeing every aspect of our lives. Lord Buddha wishes to assist every person on the Earth, shining his white light into their souls to assist them in awakening to the presence of the Creator within them, as he himself did during his many lifetimes on the Earth.

Lord Buddha is available to be invoked any time of the day. We can ask him to charge us with his light, to oversee our lives, work and spiritual growth, and he will protect and guide us with his loving hand, shielding us from negativity and guiding us forth. Lord Buddha understands everything concerning the Earth and its spiritual growth process, making him an ideal guide or spiritual mentor to invoke or call on. He is a Galactic Master; this is a title that describes the levels of initiations his soul has ascended through and the growth anchored into his being. We can be sure Lord Buddha's guidance will always be true and appropriate for our growth on the Earth. A great intensity of encouragement is sent to us from Lord Buddha, as he wishes us to connect and link with his energy to assist us in following the correct path for our growth.

Lord Buddha's ashram is an ideal place to visit either during meditation or your dream state. Simply ask to be taken to Lord Buddha's Planetary Logos Ashram on the inner planes. It is here that you can meet with him and absorb the energy of the leader of the spiritual hierarchy at a planetary level. This is a place of rest, rejuvenation, illumination, wisdom and accelerated growth. This special ashram embodies every aspect and level of the planetary hierarchy, holding within its divine energy the twelve rays of light, the wisdom of all Ascended Masters at this level and much spiritual information anchored from the solar and galactic levels of the spiritual hierarchy, appearing as a white ray of light.

There is an ascension seat that you can visit in Lord Buddha's ashram; this is a sacred light seat. While you sit upon it white light is channelled into your being. If you practise and ask to sit upon this seat during meditation or while sitting peacefully during your day you should feel the energy entering into your physical body. You will not leave your physical body but an aspect of your being will connect with this sacred seat of light and filter the energy into your physical body.

The second energy seat is a sacred garden within Lord Buddha's ashram, which is overseen by Lord Buddha and Quan Yin. This is a place of peace, tranquillity, harmony, balance and activation that can be accessed from the physical plane or on the inner planes during your sleep state. Both ascension and sacred energy seats will assist you in developing the amount of light within your physical body, as well as deepening your connection with Lord Buddha and the Twelve Buddhas who assist him.

On Earth the festival of Buddha, or the Wesak, is celebrated at the full moon in May of each year. It is a Buddhist festival that has been adopted by many light workers as an opportunity to celebrate and appreciate our Planetary Logos, Lord Buddha. This is a time when the spiritual government and hierarchy gather at the Wesak Valley in the Himalayas to receive the highest wave of energy vibration from the Creator through Lord Buddha. Lord Buddha transmits this divine energy through the trinity of the Christ Lord Maitreya, the Manu Allah Gobi and the Mahachohan Saint Germain, who channel this sacred and enlightening energy into the Earth and humanity, to raise the level of consciousness of every soul. It is a celebration of Lord Buddha's embodiment of light and wisdom on the Earth and in the spiritual planes while assisting humankind in evolving. Lord Buddha wishes us to rejoice in the manifestation of the Buddha within our physical bodies on the Earth and to ensure we are receptive to the waves of light and energy flowing from him at the time of the full moon in May or any other time of the year. We must simply ask our guides and Lord Buddha to anchor the divine and high vibrational energies descending from the Planetary Logos Ashram into our beings.

Lord Buddha is a key focus for the Earth because of his position in the planetary realm; it is he towards whom we as physical beings look to lead the way forth while we are on the Earth, and when we enter the spiritual hierarchy, either gaining a place in the spiritual government or a role elsewhere. It is a helpful practice to invoke Lord Buddha's energy each day to oversee your life, spiritual growth and path, to ensure you integrate and enact the divine plan of the Creator, receiving the correct energies within the planetary level to support your growth. If you are unsure of which energies or Masters are most needed in your life, invoke the guidance of Lord Buddha. He understands every energy, aspect and presence existing in the spiritual hierarchy at a planetary level and will assist you in forming the correct connections for your soul.

We must now gain a connection with Lord Buddha so we can resolve any blockages or problems and grasp our lessons on the Earth, allowing us to evolve to the next stage of our spiritual growth. When we allow ourselves to embody his wisdom, light and love, we will become a manifestation of the Creator on the Earth, as all are interlinked.

Accept and invoke Lord Buddha to place a white golden orb of his soul light into your heart chakra now. Let Lord Buddha balance your being so you may exist as a physical aspect of the Creator on the Earth, embodying all the divine, loving and wise qualities within the Creator's mighty soul.

'I am Buddha.'

CHAPTER 5

THE TWELVE BUDDHAS

Supporting Lord Buddha within the Planetary Logos Ashram are his Twelve Buddhas. Chosen to work alongside Lord Buddha, these twelve beings integrate not only the energies of the planetary level into their beings, but higher vibrations from within the Creator's universe to protect Lord Buddha in a bubble of the purest light.

There are many aspects to the Twelve Buddhas. They are Ascended Masters from the Earth who have gained a depth of inner peace and stillness. They sit in a circle within the Planetary Logos Ashram, meditating and connecting with the higher aspects of their beings. Their mission is to channel their energy into Lord Buddha and to energise his missions for the Earth and in the spiritual hierarchy. They create a constant flow of light, anchoring into the Planetary Logos Ashram in order to support it and ensure the highest potentials are achieved.

The Twelve Buddhas act as pillars of light. They spread an incredible peace and tranquillity into the Planetary Logos and the planetary leaders to ensure that clarity is always present within their minds. They also emanate the peace they gain from within their beings or from the core of the Creator, limitlessly across the entire universe and into the Earth. The Twelve Buddhas are a symbol of peace and harmony between every aspect of the Creator's creations. It is their stillness and oneness that labels them as Twelve Buddhas, as they are enlightenment in its purity and have evolved to exist as light without a true name.

They embody the wisdom of the universe, acting as a council or board of advisors to Lord Buddha when he needs their assistance; they offer their guidance and point out all aspects that need to be considered when Lord Buddha is required to make decisions to aid our evolution on the Earth. The Twelve Buddhas are wells of light assisting him in connecting with the will and love of the Creator. Their enlightenment and peaceful energies have been gained by the practice of constant meditation. The Twelve Buddhas were chosen from the higher levels of the spiritual hierarchy to assist Lord Buddha as Planetary Logos; their role of working in unison is a part of their growth process and allows them to ascend further. When Lord Buddha moves on to his next position and a new Planetary Logos is chosen, a new council of twelve will be selected that is compatible to work as a support network for the new leader. Their roles are very similar to our guides: they assist Lord Buddha when he invokes their energy, but otherwise they continue to emanate peace and tranquillity as constant waves throughout the Earth's universe.

Another aspect to the position of the Twelve Buddhas is their ability to hear the thoughts, prayers and cries for help that we on the Earth send up to the Creator. The Twelve Buddhas can locate us on the Earth. If we need assistance, and most importantly have asked for assistance, they then alert Lord Buddha to our situation, allowing him to send Angels or Ascended Masters to assist us as well as our personal guides. The Twelve Buddhas are vigilant to any major disasters that occur or are imminent on the Earth. While they inform Lord Buddha and the other planetary leaders, they also send waves of peace and healing from their combined energy group to resolve the situation, creating the highest vibrational result.

Lord Buddha acts as a symbol of Creator realisation to humanity and is deeply in tune with Mother Earth and her inhabitants, but the Twelve Buddhas also work with Mother Earth's vast soul, sharing their love, enlightenment and peaceful energy with her to aid her growth.

The Twelve Buddhas are connected with the twelve rays of light; they work with the Chohans and leaders of the twelve rays of light to infuse peace and their support into the work and the energies of the rays of light. They also anchor the twelve rays of light into the Planetary Logos Ashram and support the work of the Divine Director of Rays within the ashram. Every Buddha has been allocated a ray of light at a planetary level; they guide specifically the leaders or Chohans of the rays of light on Lord Buddha's behalf, anchoring his white vibration of light into the twelve Chohans. The unity between the Twelve Buddhas denotes and promotes the unity between the twelve Chohans and rays of light within the Creator's universe.

While the Twelve Buddhas mainly work to aid Lord Buddha in assisting us on the Earth, and predominately work on unseen levels, we are permitted to invoke the deep expansive and tranquil energy of the Twelve Buddhas during major problems in our lives or any kind of planetary disasters, allowing them to pour their energy of peace onto the Earth or into our bodies as healing and to build the light, love and stillness of the Creator within everything.

CHAPTER 6

MANU ALLAH GOBI

Allah Gobi holds the title of Manu on the spiritual planes; he is the head or leader of the first ray department, which is a vast, influential and powerful aspect of the spiritual hierarchy. The Manu Allah Gobi acts as an assistant or advisor to the Planetary Logos, Lord Buddha. Both work closely to devise and anchor the will or divine plans of the Creator into the first ray ashram, distributing understanding and energy to the necessary Masters, Chohans, rays and people on the Earth. The Creator's divine plans are passed down through all levels of light and Masters within the Creator's universe until they reach Lord Buddha's planetary level. The focus of the first ray of light is to express and anchor the will of the Creator into the spiritual paths, realities and journeys of students on the Earth and in the planetary level of the spiritual hierarchy.

The Manu forms the trinity with the Christ Lord Maitreya and the Mahachohan Saint Germain to support Lord Buddha's mission and to assist the spiritual development of souls on the Earth. The first three rays of light are the main ones, and the Manu holds complete responsibility over the first ray. Master El Morya assists the Manu in helping every soul to integrate with the first ray of light; understanding its divine qualities and how it can be used to aid spiritual growth. The Manu Allah Gobi's responsibilities extend beyond this as he focuses on distributing the will of the Creator to the governments and political figures on the Earth to awaken humankind through these figures; if this is not possible because many are unaware of his influences, he tries to eliminate false beliefs to bring forth the will of the Creator.

The Manu shares the divine plan of the Creator with all of humanity on the Earth, but it is only those who are receptive to his energy that will be able to understand his instructions. He is additionally in charge of the distribution of the divine plan to every level, realm, kingdom, Master and light being in our planetary level so all may work and progress with synchronicity, to evolve closer to the

43

mighty soul of the Creator, eradicating illusions and false beliefs.

The Manu and his team are so integrated and mindful of the continuous updates of the Creator's will and divine plans travelling through the spiritual levels from the higher Masters that they are instantly able to grasp the latest developments and summarise new ideas or guidance, reducing Lord Buddha's workload and guiding him appropriately. The Manu is akin to the mind of Lord Buddha and the Creator, he is constantly alert to any changes occurring in the divine plans that are already anchored onto the Earth; this allows Lord Buddha to take immediate action, always updating the will of the Creator on the Earth. The Manu Allah Gobi is not so readily available to invoke as his work is vitally important and time-consuming, but as physical beings on the Earth it is Master El Morya who is available to assist us, offering all the tools we need to comprehend the first ray of light.

The word 'Allah' means God or the Creator in the Islamic religion, while the word 'Gobi' holds a connection with the Gobi desert in Asia and a past lifetime. Allah Gobi as a soul has incarnated many times on the Earth. In his previous lifetimes he has followed the purity of the Islamic teachings, discarding any manmade beliefs, and has embodied the stillness of the Gobi desert. His lifetimes may have been the inspiration for his spiritual name. Allah Gobi is a representative of the Islamic and eastern religions in the spiritual world, the connection of the Christ and the Manu in the hierarchy symbolises the harmony that must be gained between the eastern and western civilisations and religions. All are united as one with the Creator. Their work together on the inner planes demonstrates to humankind the union that can be formed. Each religion or belief system is a tool or stepping stone to becoming united with the Creator. All are valued, but once we leave the Earth the religions of the Earth become a physical aspect and reality which are left behind; we evolve to embrace the very essence of the Creator's soul.

Allah Gobi embodies all twelve rays of light and has integrated his soul with the galactic level of the spiritual hierarchy, but his focus is now predominantly with the first ray of light which holds the power, strength, courage, passion and will of the Creator in a fiery red colour of light; through the red ray of light the will of the Creator is filtered onto the Earth. The Manu filters the guidance and instructions of Lord Buddha and the Cosmic Masters to Master El Morya and the Masters working with this ray.

The Manu is involved in team discussions or board meetings with the Christ, Mahachohan and Lord Buddha about the assignments or energy vibrations they have been given by the Creator, or need to give to humanity, to assist the evolution of the Creator's soul extensions. Many inspirational ideas and projects to assist the awakening of the Earth are explored and discussed; the wisdom that comes forth from the higher levels is not always clear. The planetary Masters must decipher the wisdom, setting it into motion through the twelve rays of light. It is the Manu who is the main advisor, other than Lord Buddha on these occasions, as he holds the deepest connection with the will of the Creator due to his role. Occasionally Masters from the higher levels join the planetary meetings to shed extra enlightenment. In the same way, the planetary leaders are invited to meetings on the solar, galactic or universal levels, to assist in the anchoring of the higher energies into the planetary level.

The Manu casts his eye over the Eastern civilisation and recruits many Masters in the spiritual realms to assist in the awakening of this area of the Earth. He is a wise and loving being devoted to assisting every person of any background or religion on the Earth, as he is able to see the truth of the soul within every physical body. The Manu is a spiritual mentor, guiding many with Master El Morya to accept and understand the will of the Creator, integrating it into their lives.

When we invoke the energy of the first ray, which will be discussed in full later, it is advisable to invoke the Manu Allah Gobi to oversee our connection, as the first ray is a powerful energy that shouldn't be used lightly. He will also assist us in embodying and discovering the Creator's will within our physical realities on the Earth.

The Manu Allah Gobi is most accomplished at embodying the peace, silence and expansion of the desert and the Creator. His understanding of stillness within the mind and body allows him to see, speak and act with the truth of the Creator, achieving and emanating true enlightenment. For those of us who meditate he holds the pinnacle of our goal for stillness. As the Manu Allah Gobi smiles graciously onto us, he permits us to call on his energy to gain a deeper meditative state than we have experienced before.

It is important for us to respect the Manu's important position as a spiritual leader, refraining from calling on him constantly throughout the day as we would our guides; we are required to follow the intuition of our souls to guide us as to when contact is necessary. We are permitted to call upon the Manu to meditate with us as a beacon of peace to encourage our inner stillness, allowing the Manu to identify the areas of our mind that need further focus and explain how to achieve profound concentration. Respect and love must be expressed to the Manu as his work is essentially important on the Earth for us as we awaken to the will and presence of the Creator within our beings and realities.

CHAPTER 7

CHRIST LORD MAITREYA

Comparable to Lord Buddha, Lord Maitreya is a Galactic Master assisting the Earth at a planetary level; he oversees the Christ Consciousness energy of a golden colour, integrating and anchoring it into the Earth. Lord Maitreya embodies the Christ Consciousness which is the pure love of the Creator. It is not directly linked to the Christian religion as its name may suggest, but describes an active consciousness of love. Accepting this energy leads to a state of awakening, living with every breath and action on the Earth as a manifestation of the Creator and love. The Christ Consciousness can affect every aspect of our bodies, from our state of minds to our emotional, physical and spiritual bodies, aligning us to the energy and light of the Creator, while nurturing our souls to merge with our physical personalities. Lord Maitreya embodies all the loving attributes we associate with the Creator; governing the Christ Consciousness, he wishes to assist us in embodying love of the purest kind.

It was through Lord Maitreya's lifetime as Bhagavan Krishna and over-lighting the Master Lord Jesus during his last few years on the Earth that he passed through his initiations of spiritual growth. He later held the position of Chohan of the second ray of light, before embracing the Christ Consciousness fully.

Lord Maitreya ensures the Christ Consciousness is readily available to those who invoke it, and acts as World Teacher of the Christ Consciousness for students in physical bodies on the Earth, and the light beings, souls and Ascended Masters on the spiritual planes at a planetary level. Lord Maitreya is a beacon of love, light and wisdom and assists many in progressing through their growth processes and initiations to step closer to complete unity with the Creator.

Lord Maitreya holds out his hands to us and wishes to lead us forth into the kingdom of the Creator. His love for humankind is immense, and as we grasp his hand, a surge of golden energy charges through our beings, assisting us in becoming a flame of love. Lord Maitreya

wishes to lead every soul along a path of love where they may understand the passion and devotion he holds for the Creator and adopt it
into their way of life. Lord Maitreya asks us to allow him to guide us
to embody the love of the Creator, which is the Christ Consciousness.
He affirms 'I am Love', and asks that we adopt this as our own mantra
and belief system. Each of us is the embodiment of love; it is Lord
Maitreya's mission to awaken us to this truth. By invoking him to
draw closer into our beings while repeating this mantra, we can attune
ourselves with his energy, allowing him to work personally with us
on our spiritual paths.

Lord Maitreya will never judge, he is a pure manifestation of love
and has walked the Earth as this manifestation; we can call on him
when meditating and ask him to channel his love into our beings and
souls to support and nurture the love within us. If we invoke his
energy, Lord Maitreya will support us with his unconditional love
when we feel fearful or insecure. As we accelerate forward on our
spiritual paths, it is valuable for us to invoke him to oversee our paths,
anchoring the Christ Consciousness into every aspect of our bodies
and realities. When we build a greater amount of love within our
bodies, we raise our consciousness significantly and are able to
connect with the truth of the Creator.

Love is desperately needed on the Earth now and Lord Maitreya
asks us to anchor the golden divine energy of the Christ Consciousness
into our beings and into the core of Mother Earth to assist her with her
spiritual acceleration. Invoke the light of the Christ Consciousness to
channel into your body each and every day; pray to Lord Maitreya to
anchor this sacred energy into your body and into the body of Mother
Earth, allowing you both to become integrated with this loving energy.
Imagine, sense or see the golden energy of love melting into your body
and aura. Lord Maitreya will be close by, caring for you as his equal
and a beloved soul of the Creator.

Most importantly, Lord Maitreya asks you to be active in your
embodiment and expression of your own inner unconditional love
and the love energy of the Creator. He asks you to love every person
on the Earth unconditionally, to emanate love as you walk, talk, eat,
drink, sleep and sit. Let every moment of your day be a moment of
love, a moment of radiating the love of the Creator. When you embody
the Christ Consciousness or the love of the Creator you become an
eternal active presence of love. Through this process you will gain

mastery and further awakening, becoming a Christ; channel of the Creator's love.

Lord Maitreya holds an ashram on the inner planes that any person can visit during their sleep state or in meditation by simply asking. When you ask to visit the ashram of the Christ you will be bathed in pure love, absorbing it into your soul with the ability to channel the energy into your physical body resting on the Earth. There will be opportunities to discuss your spiritual progress with Lord Maitreya, allowing this divine teacher to advise you. Lord Maitreya is always open to the invocations of his student on the Earth and offers his ashram as a tool to assist in the embodiment of love. Through love we can understand the truth of our mission and awaken to a greater enlightenment than we have ever experienced.

Lord Maitreya receives a great deal of energy, light and wisdom from the Planetary Logos Lord Buddha. He extracts the loving, supportive and encouraging energy from the light, integrating it with the Christ Consciousness, and channels the combined energy into the Masters of the twelve rays of light and the souls incarnated on the Earth. He assists Lord Buddha and the Mahachohan in overseeing all twelve rays of light, but he predominantly oversees the work and progress of the second ray of light because it is a smaller aspect of the Christ Ashram. A strong connection has formed between the second ray of light, the Christ and Lord Buddha, as both Masters have worked closely with the second ray energy and embody its qualities at a high vibrational level.

Lord Maitreya also places his focus on the twelfth ray of light as it is an aspect of the Christ energy and his ashram, assisting in the greater anchoring of the love of the Creator and the Christ into the Earth and the other eleven planetary rays of light.

In the western religions the Christ is a focal point of worship. Jesus Christ is seen as the son of God, a Saviour and Messiah. The Christ Consciousness which Jesus Christ embodied is overseen by Lord Maitreya. He no longer wants people to shed tears, feel fear or sympathy for his sufferings as the Master Jesus, because he is love and desires that every person embody the love of the Creator, loving each other in harmony. Lord Maitreya is a higher aspect of Master Jesus; both wish to surround the Earth in a blanket of love from the spiritual planes to anchor the Christ and love of the Creator into the Earth. When people speak of the return of the Christ, they are literally speaking of the return of love in full manifestation on the Earth.

Allow yourself to embody the Christ and love of the Creator, shining this golden energy into the darkness around you. The Christ energy is the precious jewel of the Creator's soul. Grasp the loving hand Lord Maitreya holds out for you and allow him to lead you forth to enlightenment, illumination, truth and love. Let love be your focus with every step you take on the Earth.

'I am the Christ.'

CHAPTER 8
MAHACHOHAN SAINT GERMAIN

When invoking Saint Germain he will supportively place his hands on your shoulders and channel his energy into your being. This is a high vibrational energy that integrates the violet cleansing flame of light as well as all twelve rays of light.

Saint Germain's energy is very powerful, divine and loving. He holds a great healing ability within his amazing light body as well as being accomplished in many different aspects and spiritual skills. He is wise, deeply connected to the love and light of the Creator, and devoted to humankind. Saint Germain is titled the Mahachohan, governor of the extension rays of light in our spiritual hierarchy on a planetary level, and works alongside the Christ and the Manu. He is a respected figure due to his achievements in ascension and the tuition he offers his students.

Saint Germain's name stems from a French region on the Earth, 'Saint Germain' to which the Mahachohan was the royal count. The count's last lifetime on the Earth was truly remarkable, as not only was he a manifestation of light and love but he discovered the wondrous magic and skills of his soul, integrating it into his life for many to see. An amazing ability he possessed was to remove the boundaries of physical death from his reality and continue living well beyond the average age on the Earth. Saint Germain has had many lifetimes on the Earth, making a great contribution to life as we now recognise it today, as, for example Christopher Columbus, Francis Bacon (or William Shakespeare), and Merlin.

Saint Germain has many followers because of his vast knowledge, wisdom and variety of skills. The Master governed the seventh ray of light of a violet colour while discovering the violet flame of transmutation and its cleansing uses for humanity. Most recently he has evolved to hold the position of Mahachohan. As with all the roles in the spiritual hierarchy, this is not simply a title of honour or respect but holds a great deal of responsibility. The Mahachohan Saint

Germain oversees the third ray of light while guiding and instructing the Masters of the other four rays of light within the planetary level. The four to seven rays of light are an extension of the third ray of light. The third ray of light is of a yellow colour and promotes active and spiritual intelligence and manifestation.

Master Serapis Bey is the Chohan or Master of this ray, working alongside Saint Germain to anchor and manifest the third ray of light onto the Earth and within the souls of humanity.

Saint Germain's responsibilities are immense as each ray has its own projects, qualities and purposes which are unique and diverse to the others. The Masters work together; there is no ray of light or ashram that is better than the others, or neglected, as everyone understands their focus and the unity existing between them. It is one of Saint Germain's missions to ensure everything runs to the plans of the Creator and Cosmic Masters, and that each ray is used to its highest potential for the good of humankind. It could be said that Saint Germain resembles a head of many departments, overseeing numerous subject matters for the headmaster, Lord Buddha.

Saint Germain still holds within his being the divine qualities of the seventh ray of light to which he was Chohan, and continues to remain a Master of the violet flame. He holds a deep connection with it as he accessed its energy for our use on the Earth. The violet flame is a cleansing flame of light that burns up negative energy, emotions and thought patterns, freeing a soul from their effects. It is a potent flame of light that should only be experienced for short periods of time each day coupled with a nurturing energy of love, but its results are wondrous.

Anyone can invoke the presence of Saint Germain, asking him to oversee a healing process with the violet flame. The violet flame of light will then descend from the seventh ray ashram where it rests, running over and down your body slowly until it reaches the bottom of your energy field before returning in the same way it came. It will burn up any unwanted and unneeded energy so that they no longer influence your actions or cause blockages.

You can call on Saint Germain and the violet flame of light to assist you when you are ill, or feeling low in energy or in mood. The flame will remove any blockages that are causing problems, but it is your responsibility then to invoke the healing energy of the angels to run the love of the Creator through your being to fill any gaps left in your aura or energy systems. We must respect the Mahachohan's responsibilities. He is devoted to the Earth, but if he is unavailable to assist us then Lady Portia, the new Chohan of the violet ray of light, will aid us in this healing and cleansing process.

Saint Germain holds the department of Active Intelligence. His role with the assistance of Master Serapis Bey is to bring the energy of divine intelligence associated with the will of the Creator to the trinity that assists Lord Buddha. Saint Germain acts as a channel for Lord Buddha's and the Creator's mind, sending this divine and needed energy to the Earth while manifesting the celestial and influential thoughts of the Creator onto the Earth. In his position of Mahachohan he is known for his incredible ability to do this. It is his purpose to teach every extension soul of the Creator's mighty soul to manifest their desires and realities using the power of their minds. He uses the third ray energy as his fuel to manifest the qualities of the eleven other rays of Creator's light onto the Earth in many different aspects, vibrations and levels. In truth, although the Mahachohan oversees the rays three to seven, he also aids all rays of light in anchoring their energy into the Earth and the souls of humanity.

The trinity of ashrams governed by the Manu, Christ and Mahachohan are the Earth's support network and our guiding light. They symbolise that these three qualities of will, love and divine intelligence or manifestation are the qualities most honoured by the Creator, and they therefore have much to teach us. It is our mission to embody all three rays while on the Earth and use them in our daily lives so we may act, think and love as the Creator manifested on the Earth.

These three Masters hold such remarkable positions in the spiritual government that it is impossible for us as physical beings to truly grasp their purpose and influence on our Earth. I believe that it is important and comforting to know we are not alone on the Earth. Not only do we have personal guides to attend to our individual needs but we have a spiritual hierarchy consisting of many intricate levels of light beings watching over the Earth, its progress and our development. Let us take the support and love offered to us by the Manu, the Christ, the Mahachohan and Lord Buddha, knowing with faith that we are safe, protected, and that the cosmic thread of the Creator is intertwined with every aspect of the Earth. Let us honour the planetary leaders and their assistants working with them by invoking their energy to aid our spiritual development, respecting them by focusing our minds on the light of the Creator, learning from the demonstrations and examples they offer us.

Allow Saint Germain to assist you in connecting with the special energy of the third ray of light and its extension rays. He will clarify the rays of light for you, helping you to choose which would be most valuable in your current spiritual growth. Saint Germain is such a wise, magical and evolved being of light that you may call on his energy to expand and enlighten your mind, drawing new spiritual skills from within your being. He will assist you in casting away the limited thoughts caused by Earth's physicality to gain an insight into the power of your soul, the beacon of light within you.

'I am the manifestation of the Creator.'

CHAPTER 9

WORLD TEACHERS

In the past there appears to have been only one or maybe two Masters occupying the position and ashram of World Teacher. This position still remains within the spiritual hierarchy, but when we connect into the spiritual planes we discover there are many spiritual teachers we can access. In fact, nearly all Ascended Masters and light beings are teachers as they have a burning desire within them to educate and inspire others to grasp the same truths they understand. All the Archangels also act as teachers for many students across the world. Every Master is unique, they all have their special ways of enlightening us; we are also unique and are attracted to the souls on the inner planes who have a similar perceptive to us. In truth, we could say every Master, Extraterrestrial Being or Archangel is a World Teacher because they all have their students and followers over whom they watch and to whom they channel further wisdom.

All the planetary leaders are World Teachers because of the devotion they hold to assisting us on the Earth and the variety of subject matters and qualities they anchor into their beings from the Creator. The titles given to the Masters within the spiritual hierarchy are simply labels portraying their responsibilities. These titles are not important but help us to understand their roles further. Many channels and light workers give a variety of labels or titles to our planetary leaders and a diversity of Masters as our leaders; this is due to their different backgrounds and education, as well as the great volume of Masters wishing to assist us. It is important for us to focus on connecting and receiving energy in whichever way is appropriate for us, rather than allowing their labels to confuse us.

It is important for our spiritual hierarchy that we have a leader of education to ensure we all follow the divine plan of growth from the Creator. There are numerous paths of education we may follow to achieve our soul's goals and unity with the Creator; this is why a World Teacher has been appointed as an overseer of every educational path available to humankind. Most recently the position of World Teacher has been shared by Master Kuthumi and Master Sananda. In our hearts Master Kuthumi will always be our World Teacher, but his growth has enabled him to move forth along his spiritual path. It is Master Sananda who has taken over full responsibility of the role after progressing from the position of Chohan of the sixth ray of light.

A World Teacher basically holds the beacon of light of spiritual education for humanity, helping us to awaken from our physical realities and receive or access the correct information, teachings, practices and techniques to aid our spiritual evolution and development processes.

As the Earth develops and rises in consciousness, new Masters are taking their place alongside Master Sananda as extensions of the World Teacher position. The teachings of these Masters are already popular with humanity, the wisdom and enlightenment they have to offer is diverse. The volume of people awakening on the Earth is resulting in an increase in Master Sananda's work and so additional Masters are gathering to share the work, uniting their teaching, practices and students as one in the name of the Creator.

There are seven additional Masters who have become extensions of the World Teacher Ashram; among these Masters are Master Djwhal Khul, Native American Indian White Eagle, Native American Indian Silver Birch, Lord Rama and Master Thoth. The two other teachers have yet to be revealed to humanity as Master Sananda declares that we as a civilisation have not yet developed to the appropriate level of awareness, mindset or light to accept the presences of the remaining two Masters. There will come a time in the future when the names of the two teachers will be revealed to us on the Earth. The work and teachings of the first five teachers are significant to our current evolution on the Earth; consequently there is a need for us to accept their presence and positions in the spiritual hierarchy.

Master Djwhal Khul is already respected as one of the wisest Ascended Masters. He currently tutors the largest volume of students, as his loving and kind nature resonates with many on the Earth. His knowledge is varied and thorough, helping us to gain information on many subject matters rather than focusing on one spiritual area at the early states of our growth. Master Djwhal Khul constantly inspires us at every stage of spiritual evolution, ensuring we remain focused. He is the main Extension World Teacher.

Native American Indians White Eagle and Silver Birch have been selected because of the advanced teachings they have to share with humanity in relation to connecting and working with the Earth. Both Masters wish to assist us in honouring our lives, our residence here and the soul of Mother Earth. Their teachings and techniques enable us to live and grow in harmony with Mother Earth, to raise our planetary conscious level, rather than battling against her beloved energy. They wish to awaken our minds to the harm we are causing Mother Earth and our own souls, assisting us in transforming negative situations, helping us to view the beauty of Mother Earth and the Creator manifested on the Earth once more. In order for us to ascend and develop there is a need for us to respect and unite with Mother Earth.

Lord Rama is a wise Ascended Master who teaches the same lectures and methods as were revealed in the mystery schools of long lost civilisations on the Earth and on the inner planes. He aids us in discovering ancient talents and skills that will serve us in our spiritually evolving civilisations on the Earth. He helps us to access past memories and wisdom which will assist us to make major transformations in the physical way we live our lives. He focuses on bringing natural technology back to the Earth that nurtures the soul while helping us survive, rather than poisoning our energy systems.

Master Thoth is an aspect of Lord Buddha's soul; Lord Buddha takes on many forms within the Creator's universe. Master Thoth is a wise and accomplished Egyptian god, noted for inventing writing for the Egyptian civilisation. He is equipped in all subjects that aid spiritual and psychic development; we may study with Master Thoth in his Temple of Learning, which is an extension of the World Teacher Ashram.

The seven World Teachers have evolved beyond the planetary level and vibrate at a higher level of existence in the spiritual hierarchy, but they wish to assist with the huge volume of souls developing on the Earth. These seven Masters will now take care of the demands for spiritual enlightenment that we make from the Earth.

The presence of seven new Masters overseeing our spiritual education and the wisdom that our guides offer us is very exciting as it signifies that our knowledge will expand dramatically because of the vast awareness these Masters hold between them. It also indicates we have many teachers to choose from, ensuring we gain a thorough and expansive spiritual awareness. We must not be concerned about which Master is most suitable for our growth process as it is most likely we will always be attracted to the Master or World Teacher who is most appropriate to assist our individual growth process on the Earth.

There are spiritual teachers on all levels of the spiritual hierarchy; a solar teacher, galactic teacher, universal teacher, multi-universal teacher and cosmic teacher, all aiding the growth process of the soul extensions of the Creator. Each ensures we receive the perfect lessons, information and understandings at the correct times on our spiritual journey on the Earth and in the spiritual universe. They oversee the speed we evolve at and assist us in anchoring and accessing wisdom from the universe and our souls in order to support the expansion of light and love within our bodies. Let us invoke Master Sananda as World Teacher of the planetary level to guide us forth.

CHAPTER 10

WORLD TEACHER, MASTER SANANDA

Master Sananda has lived many lifetimes on the Earth. His most notable past lifetimes were as Adam, Joseph, Amilius, a Melchizedek, Apollonius of Tyanna and Jesus. It was through his embodiment as Jesus that Master Sananda expressed the devotional quality of the sixth ray of light, the loving wisdom of the second ray of light and the Christ Consciousness to people on Earth. Master Sananda allowed himself to be overshadowed by his higher aspect Lord Maitreya, thus anchoring the pure qualities of the second ray and the Christ Consciousness into his soul.

Master Jesus is an aspect or past life incarnation of Master Sananda's soul. The two are therefore the same, but when we invoke either we will notice the difference in the qualities that they hold, which is akin to the different personalities of a human. Master Sananda originates from the planet Venus, our sister planet, where the entire civilisation holds the focus of love. Master Sananda shared the love his soul absorbed from his home with us on the Earth during several of his incarnations. He continues to work with and embody the love of the Creator as he takes full responsibility of the World Teacher position, overseeing the spiritual education of our planet.

This is not a new position for Master Sananda as he has shared the responsibilities of World Teacher with Master Kuthumi for some time. As Master Kuthumi evolves to his next stage of growth, Master Sananda steps forward to embody the role. With the new presences of the seven Extension World Teachers at his side, Master Sananda now has many Masters to share the workload and tasks of the World Teacher. As the main World Teacher Master Sananda observes and oversees the new Masters ensuring they receive the divine plan of the Creator that he acquires from Lord Maitreya. Master Sananda's position has now evolved because of the presence of the seven Masters supporting his mission of education. He now appears as the headmaster of education for Earth school, ensuring students of the Earth connect with his energy or one of the seven World Teachers, in order to receive the illumination and awareness that is needed for ascension from the Earth and to rise in consciousness.

Most students or light workers on the Earth do not realise they are connected to the World Teachers as it is their guides that ensure the connection is manifested. Some students do not recognise that one of their personal guides can be a World Teacher for our planetary level. We must remember that every soul is interconnected and it is not a coincidence when we meet people with similar guides to us, it signifies we are enrolled as students of these Masters and their educational departments.

The World Teacher Master Sananda is the personal guide to every soul on the Earth, he is the guiding thread of light that illuminates our minds and draws us to gain greater enlightenment. The seven Extension World Teachers are also our personal guides and tutors, but because of our different missions or lessons on the Earth, we resonate more with some Masters than others. If we observed our many lifetimes on the Earth we might see that within each lifetime we resonate with different teachers. This is because of the various processes of growth that need to be achieved.

Before accepting his current position Master Sananda was the Chohan of the sixth ray of light, which is of an indigo colour. It is a devotional energy and one of the purest forms of acceptance of the Creator's manifestation. The indigo ray is divine and inspirational, working as an instigator to assist students in uniting with every aspect of the Creator's soul. It is a ray that builds inner faith in ourselves and in the presence of the Creator; this is of course a quality that Master Sananda and Lord Maitreya bestowed on us when in manifestation as Jesus.

Lady Nada, who is the feminine aspect of Master Sananda, governs the eighth ray of light of cleansing qualities, helping us to appreciate the many qualities that Master Sananda brings to his position of World Teacher. He is able to teach us to love the Creator and each other with sincerity and trust; he can tutor in the importance of cleansing and healing as well as anchoring the Christ Consciousness, among various other subjects. Master Sananda profoundly embodies and emanates the first three rays of light, aiding us in accepting the will, love and manifestation skills of the Creator into our hearts.

Love is the essence of his being. His passion for the Creator is immense and he shares this openly with his students as well as teaching us the importance of devotion to our studies, enlightenment and spiritual paths. Master Sananda opens the book of truth within us, allowing the spiritual wisdom to be released. All the practices, techniques and wisdom Master Sananda presents to us are already within our beings, he is not teaching us but assisting us in remembering once more. We are all evolved beings and spiritual teachers, it is just that we are yet to remember or realise this. Master Sananda assists us in our awakening practices and aids us in processing the wisdom of our souls and the Creator in our physical minds. He expands our memory so we may comprehend our past existences, lifetimes and the insights gained, to aid our current evolution.

Master Sananda is the teacher or tutor of every receptive person on the Earth regardless of their background, beliefs or religious values. He constantly emanates wisdom, spiritual insights and love into every aspect of the world. We as humans automatically inhale the wise light without realising, as it is integrated into our air and atmosphere, helping us to evolve to a stage where we may comprehend Master Sananda as a teacher and call on his energy to illuminate our minds. We can open our energy systems to receive the constant flow of wisdom Master Sananda radiates from his ashram on the inner planes. Asking Master Sananda to direct his wise illumination into our beings each day will accelerate our growth tremendously. As light workers we can accept and channel Master Sananda's energy into our surroundings and the people we meet, placing ourselves as anchors on the Earth of the spiritual educational vibration of light from Master Sananda's ashram. When we are confused or in need of advice for our lives or situations on the Earth, it is Master Sananda we can consult, asking him to share his wise evolved soul and enlightenment with our minds and hearts on the Earth.

Master Sananda holds an ashram we may all visit during our sleep states or meditations to study and be guided by the Master himself. New additional ashrams as extensions of the World Teacher Ashram are now materialising as the seven new World Teachers build ashrams and places of study from their soul light. The World Teacher Ashram is emerging as a vast spiritual school that we may explore, visiting each ashram while developing a connection with the spiritual teachers of our planet. Let us take advantage of this inspirational new school on the inner planes that is expanding to accommodate our needs.

CHAPTER 11

MASTER KUTHUMI

When Master Kuthumi answers the call of his students, he appears with a large smile on his face and a joyous energy vibrating from his being. He truly embodies the loving qualities of the second ray of light. His energy is uplifting, reassuring and supportive with warmth in his words of wisdom. Master Kuthumi is an evolved spiritual Master at a galactic level and assists many on the Earth with their spiritual growth. He is known as the World Teacher because of the vast volumes of students on the Earth following his teachings. Master Kuthumi still works as World Teacher, but after working alongside Master Sananda for a lengthy period of time he has given sole respon-sibility of the World Teacher Ashram to him.

Throughout his lifetimes on the Earth Master Kuthumi embodied the love and wisdom of the second ray: as Pythagoras, as a wise man at the birth of Jesus, a disciple of Jesus in his later years, and Saint Francis of Assisi. In his incarnation as Saint Francis he demonstrated a great connection with Mother Earth and the animal kingdom with the ability to communicate through the love of his soul. He verified to the world that animals react to love in the same way humans do, but still even in this developed world we are unable to protect and love our wild animals, continuing to sacrifice their love for our own needs. Master Kuthumi intertwined his thread of love into humanity while on the Earth, but it is his presence in the spiritual hierarchy that is inspiring many light workers.

We couldn't ask for a more loving spiritual teacher. He is kind, gentle but firm in his teaching and assists in the development of many spiritual children on the Earth awakening to their souls at a young age. Master Kuthumi embodies the divine qualities of all three main rays of light, but his heart remains with the second ray of light where he held the position of Chohan, working alongside Master Djwhal Khul. There was talk of Master Kuthumi evolving to become the next soul to embody the Christ Ashram, but as on Earth, the thread of change is a large part of the spiritual hierarchy and Master Kuthumi has chosen to move to the star of Sirius within the constellation of Canis Major. He wishes to advance beyond his current awareness and is following a path of tuition on Sirius with the resident Masters. His evolved nature allows him to study and lecture on the star of Sirius, to assist with the growth of the souls already resident at the school and the souls that visit during their sleep state from the Earth and other planets. He is making a great impression on the inhabitants of Sirius as he expands his spiritual wisdom to assist his students in gaining a greater clarity and understanding. Many of Master Kuthumi's students and followers now travel to the star of Sirius to continue their tuition with him; he would never abandon his students, they – or we – are so precious to him. He simply hungers for growth and additional wisdom to expand his soul energy.

Sirius holds an advancement school; it is a place of learning that prepares the Masters who have ascended from the Earth to obtain greater roles in the spiritual hierarchy, and the students of the Earth to ascend. It is similar to a college or university on the Earth, helping its students to achieve their soul's desires and goals. Sirius is a path of education that many follow once they have graduated from Earth school. A variety of lessons and lectures can be attended on a vast mixture of subject matters that we as yet may not be able to grasp in our physical forms. Masters can choose lessons that will allow them to progress along a particular path, while lecturing to other students in their specialised field. Not all Masters have the chance to lecture.

The star and Great White Lodge of Sirius has a great influence on the Earth. It is the eighth nearest star to us and obtains its energy and light from the Galactic Core and the Universal Logos Melchizedek, which is one of the reasons it appears as the brightest star in our night sky: it holds the light of a cosmic level and the energy of the Creator. This is why it is a school that countless Masters are eager to attend. Many Sirians communicate with channels and light workers on the Earth. We may view them as Extraterrestrials but their star and the opportunities they offer us make them a valued part of our spiritual hierarchy.

During my communications with Master Kuthumi, he reassures me he is completely devoted to the Earth, humanity and his students. He watches over his students and those who invoke his presence or wisdom on the Earth, always responding to their calls. His connection with humanity is as strong as ever. He explains that his change of position from Chohan of the second ray of light to World Teacher didn't alter anything for the light workers on the Earth. He has broken away from the title of World Teacher but not the role; again, everything will remain the same for us on the Earth. It just allows his soul to grow and expand to achieve a greater awareness.

If we wish to speak with Master Kuthumi then we must simply call his name and ask him to surround us in his energy, explaining how we wish him to help us. He will always graciously answer our calls. Master Kuthumi opens his heart to light beings on the Earth and invites us to visit him on the Sirian star, known as the Sirius Lodge, where the Sirian Great White Lodge of Ascended Masters is in residence, to connect with his energy, obtain guidance, or really for any spiritual reason.

In truth, although Master Sananda has taken on the responsibilities of World Teacher, overseeing the educational progress of humanity, Master Kuthumi will always act as a World Teacher to the Earth and humanity, as he allows himself to be receptive to our calls, wishing to remain an integral part of our lives, growth and spiritual education on the Earth. He is our father, brother and friend. We may visit during our sleep states on the Earth or during meditation. Master Kuthumi gives us permission to invoke his presence to our sides whenever we need to; this is a gracious invitation and comfort to know.

Visiting Master Kuthumi suggests we will be able to visit the Sirius Lodge, with the potential of enrolling in some lectures under our soul's guidance and Master Kuthumi's wise instructions, while anchoring the Ascended Master consciousness of the Great White Lodge. The energy and important teachings of the school of Sirius is one of the reasons Master Kuthumi has relocated to this star, so that his students may benefit from the resident teachers as an addition to the educational programs of the World Teachers. Sirius is an essential part of our evolution process and is now enhancing its presence on the Earth to aid our development.

Master Kuthumi is recognised as being accomplished in channelling through light beings on the Earth and is known for working with new channels to instigate, develop and expand their skills of channelling with confidence. If you wish to begin to channel the divine energy and wisdom of the Masters, Angels or Archangels on the inner planes, have problems while channelling, need to widen or develop your channel, then Master Kuthumi is definitely the Master to invoke as he has worked with numerous channels on the Earth of all stages of awareness. He will oversee the building of your channel when you ask him to and will channel his words of wisdom into your mind when you are ready. Master Kuthumi understands the correct amount of light that is needed to build and maintain a channel and will joyously practise your channelling abilities with you to strengthen your connection with the spiritual world. He is known then to bring new Masters or light souls forward to connect with you and to expand your repertoire as a channel.

It is valuable to remember that Master Kuthumi has a wonderful ability of working with children, whether they have awoken to their souls or not. He can soothe troubled and problematic souls while encouraging shy souls to express themselves lovingly and securely. Master Kuthumi can be invoked to assist in the spiritual and physical aspects of a child, helping them to adjust to and achieve the most out of their lives on the Earth.

Additionally he is accomplished in placing golden orbs of light in the aura, containing valuable information for a soul to access and discover. It is because of his ability and devotion to assist us in any aspect of our lives on the Earth that he has been in the past, and still remains, a spiritual teacher and educator of high esteem in the planetary spiritual hierarchy.

Call on Master Kuthumi, with his loving wise energy. You will receive the correct spiritual education for your being whether it is accessed from the spiritual or physical planes.

CHAPTER 12

EXTENSION WORLD TEACHER MASTER DJWHAL KHUL

Master Djwhal Khul is an Ascended Master of radiant light with a tremendous knowledge and understanding of spiritual matters. If you are confused while exploring spiritual wisdom then Master Djwhal Khul is the Master to call on; he is esteemed for the wisdom and enlightenment that he has attained.

Master Djwhal Khul lived on the Earth alongside Kuthumi and El Morya, together the three wise men at the birth of Jesus. In other lives he was Confucius, and later an assistant to Kuthumi, who incarnated as Pythagoras. As a Tibetan monk, Master Djwhal Khul was the creator of the Tibetan foundation.

It is not his lifetimes or presence on the Earth that are incredible in this case, but his achievements in the spiritual planes. Master Djwhal Khul is a beloved teacher and has assisted many souls incarnate on the Earth from his position on the inner planes; he has channelled his wisdom into many spiritual books, notably through Alice Bailey. He also assisted Master Joshua in his development and ascension on the Earth from the Synthesis Ashram.

Master Djwhal Khul is an excellent source to consult to discover the truth, and this is why so many people have connected with his energy and presence all over the world. He is a great figure in ascension because of his unconditional devotion and love for the souls on the Earth and our spiritual growth process.

For a lengthy period Master Djwhal Khul worked as a Chohan of the Synthesis Ashram on the second ray of light, assisting many students to integrate the divine and planetary energies of the Creator into their physical beings on the Earth. His presence in the Synthesis Ashram was very popular, resulting in a great following of his teachings; even now Ascended Masters consult Master Djwhal Khul when they are in need of assistance as his wisdom is profound.

Master Djwhal Khul embodies the wisdom and loving energy of the second ray of light and for a while acted as Chohan for the ray to allow Master Kuthumi to resume new positions. He still acts as a guide for Master Joshua, current Chohan of the second ray of light, assisting with the training of the new Masters on the second ray, while also working closely with Lord Buddha to enhance the awakening of souls on the Earth. He keeps a watchful eye over many places and projects in the spiritual hierarchy at a planetary and solar level, continuing to teach and assist the Masters on the inner planes with their growth. It is because of his interest in many projects concerning the Earth and inner planes that he is akin to an open spiritual book that we may access to expand our minds further.

Master Djwhal Khul has worked closely with the World Teachers for some time; he was the first Extension World Teacher to be selected because of his connection with Master Sananda and Master Kuthumi, and his profound comprehension of the Creator's universe. He has accepted the position of Extension World Teacher with passion and delight as it enables him to assist so many more students. Connecting with Master Djwhal Khul is a great honour; his participation in our lives will only lead to positive results in our spiritual growth processes.

Djwhal Khul's most trusted and beloved friend is the Master Kuthumi; each assisted the other in their evolution especially while they were on the Earth. It was Master Kuthumi who assisted him in ascending from his lifetime as a Tibetan Monk or Master. Both have worked closely on the inner planes, and although Master Kuthumi has evolved to the star Sirius for extra growth, Master Djwhal Khul dedicates some of his time to his own studies while also delivering lectures on the star of Sirius, ensuring he has a wealth of knowledge to share with his students.

Master Djwhal Khul can be visited in his ashram which is an extension of the World Teacher Ashram and can be invoked during meditation. Repeating his name is a powerful way of calling on his energy. He will assist us with anything we ask of him; his aim is to offer enlightenment to humankind and to share the love of the Creator. He is a quiet man of peace and tranquillity; he will not speak unless he has something to share. His focus is crystal clear when it comes to his own spiritual development and the advancement of others. He will lovingly come straight to the core of all matters, offering us what we need to understand or grasp rather than what we believe we need for our growth. He has assisted so many light beings on the Earth to master their bodies and anchor the love of the Creator into their beings.

Master Djwhal Khul could be seen as a father figure of spiritual education for our planet. We can invoke Master Djwhal Khul to assist us in connecting with the second ray of light and with the twelve rays of light available at a planetary level, as well as planning our spiritual education and illumination with us. His techniques of teaching and guiding souls to the point at which they wish to ascend is renowned.

Master Djwhal Khul also has a tremendous ability to cleanse, clear and remove negative energy, thought patterns and emotions from any soul who asks for his assistance in a cleansing and healing process. He discovered the Fear Matrix Removal Program which can be experienced in the Synthesis Ashram of the second ray of light and allows souls to remove the effects and influences of fear in their realities, bodies and souls. Simply ask Master Djwhal Khul to enrol you in this program and to assist you in removing all fears and their causes from every aspect of your being. To support this work you can ask to visit the Synthesis Ashram at night to benefit from the Fear Matrix Removal Program that is continuously running in the Synthesis Ashram. Djwhal Khul ensures that the Masters working in the Synthesis Ashram will bathe you in light and guide you to release any negative habits that may be causing blockages in your energy systems. We all must release the pain of our past and the influence of the physical world on our souls in order to discover the truth.

Master Djwhal Khul's love is radiant and it would be a missed opportunity not to invoke him to oversee our spiritual paths, development and cleansing processes on the Earth. He offers us much wisdom to help us understand our realities and lessons, as well as opening our minds and hearts to the spiritual world that is our true home. When we invoke Master Djwhal Khul to assist our spiritual growth, he enrols us as his student into his World Teacher Ashram and program of education, keeping a watchful eye on our progress, coming to our aid when it is needed. His ashram is always filled with students who visit in their sleep states. When we visit we can connect with his other students to assist us in acknowledging and accepting our oneness and unity with all manifestations of the Creator. Master Djwhal Khul enjoys visiting his students when they are consciously awake on the Earth as this builds a deeper bond and connection, ensuring we do not overlook any experiences or possibilities of growth that can be gained in Earth school.

It is essential for us to honour Master Djwhal Khul for his participation and focus in our evolution on the Earth, as a civilisation and as individuals. From his position within the World Teacher Ashram Master Djwhal Khul offers a helping hand to all who wish to climb the spiritual ladder.

CHAPTER 13

THE BOARD OF KARMA

Karma is an energy, vibration or light we receive and create because of our actions on the Earth. We can receive positive Karma, appearing as a vibrant or divine shade of light within our beings, or we can receive negative karma, visible within the aura as a dark or murky energy or colour of light. This depends on where our minds are focused. The Board of Karma is a part of the spiritual hierarchy existing at a planetary level. It is a group of Ascended Masters, Goddesses and light beings who are devoting some of their energy to assisting physical beings with their karmic issues. They work to release the effects of negative karma or energy from the physical, emotional and mental bodies. Their focus is on removing and resolving negative karma rather than accepting positive karma, because it is easier for us to accept positive energy from our situations than to release negative energy.

When a person hurts us in any way we can feel pain on numerous levels. The negative energy and memory of the situation, however large or small, remains within our energy systems until we consciously make a decision to remove it. If on the other hand we are the person causing harm or pain through our actions to another human or animal, we will embody a negative energy as a result of our actions. This negative energy can manifest as guilt or shame. Some people even bury their negative emotions, fears and thoughts deep within their being, as a way of dealing with the energy. This causes more pain for everyone involved in the negative situation, as they are connected through the experience.

Storing the energy and memories within the energy systems produces blockages, stagnant energy and eventually illness. Many people's fears and illnesses are caused by the memories and energy of negative situations remaining in their auras. It doesn't matter whether we were a victim or the person inflicting harm, all our actions and thoughts either cause a negative or positive energy that remains within our beings. It is therefore important for us to understand the way our minds work, programming our thoughts to emanate love. Most karmic issues are due to unprogrammed minds as well as the power and influence of the ego when we are not connected to the love of the Creator.

Some of us can carry karmic issues with us through many lifetimes because we are not prepared to face up to our actions. We have the power and tools to deal with our own karma, the negative emotions and thoughts that are held within our beings and energy systems, but because most of us are yet to realise this, there are dedicated Masters and light beings working in the spiritual hierarchy to assist us in cleansing our bodies.

People experience the effects of karma every day without realising it, but as we evolve spiritually and awaken to the light, we have a greater awareness of how our actions not only affect our own wellbeing and energy vibrations but influence the spiritual energy vibrations of Earth's entire civilisation, because we are so closely interlinked. When we harm someone even with our judging minds, we feel the pain caused at a deeper level because we have become more sensitive to the energies of others. It is during these times that we can call on the members of the Board of Karma to assist us with healing, releasing the situation and its causes from our beings and from the other person or people involved. The Board of Karma focuses on souls incarnate on the Earth because this is where negativity and karma is most evident. By the time we have evolved from the Earth into our light bodies, all karmic issues have been released and dissolved because of the greater amount of light anchoring into our beings.

The members of the Board of Karma are predominantly healers. They allow the life force energy of the Creator to flow through their energy bodies to assist people to remove their negative baggage, freeing the soul to evolve and expand spiritually. They will assist anyone who invokes their energy for healing. Even the Archangels and Ascended Masters offering healing to a physical being call on members of the Board of Karma to resolve stubborn karmic issues that are not dissolving with the power of their healing energy.

It is a wise practice to invoke the members of the Board of Karma to heal and resolve any negative karmic issues that may be stagnating within our beings each week during meditation. A simple invocation to the Board of Karma explaining that we wish to be released of any negative karmic energies or issues that are currently hindering our growth will attract a compatible member of the Board of Karma to work with us and begin to heal our beings. By invoking this healing and releasing process each week, we can delve down deeper into the layers of our emotions, energy systems and thought patterns to shine light into every aspect of our beings. Asking for help from the Karmic Board will accelerate our growth tremendously and will allow us to release any unwanted energy in a safe and secure atmosphere filled with light. This process will allow us to gain the most out of our lifetimes on the Earth, free from recurring lessons entering into our lives and remaining unresolved.

If you are aware of recurring lessons in your life and you are having trouble understanding them or their place in your reality, then call on the Board of Karma to work with you to bring clarity and to bathe you in healing energy. Sometimes simply becoming aware of a recurrent negative pattern or experience in your life is enough to bring closure to the lesson.

Their work is vitally important for the spiritual growth of a physical person on the Earth. Most of the members are of a feminine energy; it is their nourishing energy that causes such transformational effects in resolving and removing karma of any negative nature. Lady Portia, Lady Nada, Lady Mary, Lady Quan Yin, Pallas Athena and even Lady Vessa Andromeda all work on the Board of Karma to assist humanity.

More people on the Earth now wish to deal with, heal and resolve their negative karmic issues; the rise in humanity's consciousness implies there is need for the Board of Karma to recruit extra helpers to assist their cause. Each member represents and anchors different rays of light into the united energy of the Board of Karma; in addition they anchor the energy of the Karmic Board into the ray they represent. Lady Quan Yin explains that the ray of light each member represents does not always marry with the ray they are a Chohan of or work with, as there are many aspects to their spiritual mission. The Board of Karma allows them to work with alternative rays, to anchor a different energy into their being and the ray ashram they work with. She understands that this can be confusing for light workers on the Earth, but her work on the Board of Karma is an extended aspect of her soul's mission. It is similar to holding several positions or jobs on the Earth; each position assists in the growth of the soul in different ways.

When asking who else works on the Board of Karma, Quan Yin advises us to focus instead on invoking the energy of the whole Board. When we do so, the appropriate member of the Board will draw close to assist us in our healing process. As a result we will receive the most helpful energy and Master. Each of us has the ability to connect and communicate with the energy of the member who is assisting us; we can discover their name, if we wish. Lady Quan Yin reveals that there are many Masters and light beings who work invisibly for the Board of Karma; many wish to remain anonymous as this allows them to devote their energy to assisting those who invoke the healing light of the Board of Karma.

When we focus on resolving our negative karmic issues we must allow ourselves to open our energy systems to become receptive to the positive karma that flows into our beings. Positive karma will be attracted to us due to our loving and positive thoughts, our caring hearts and the love and light we emanate. As we focus on our own spiritual growth process we naturally open our beings to receiving positive karma, which raises our energy vibrations and assists us in connecting on a deeper level with the source of the Creator. We need to invoke the Board of Karma to intervene in our lives, helping us to clear any past negative karma so we may be free to receive the abundant positive karmic energies of the Creator deep into our physical personalities, realities and souls to raise our vibrations.

PART 2

THE TWELVE RAYS OF LIGHT

CHAPTER 14

An Introduction to
The Twelve Rays of Light

Our universe is comprised of energy; energy is our essence, our fuel and source of life. Each physical being and soul, whether human, animal, insect or plant, originates as energy. Even our surroundings are created from energy that derives from the Creator's larger soul and can be described as love or light. Within the Creator's energy is a vast variety of qualities, vibrations and expressions.

This energy can be sensed, seen, heard or even grasped if it vibrates at a low frequency visible as a physical aspect. We can compare this to the highest vibration of light that exists within the core of the Creator, which is of a clear or invisible colour. In between the solid energy or light visible on the Earth and the clear energy of the Creator are many different levels, dimensions and vibrations of light and energy that we must explore, accept and anchor into our souls in order to ascend to become united with the Creator.

There are numerous expressions and vibrations of the Creator's soul, but we are presented with twelve main qualities to aid our learning and discovery at a planetary level. All twelve rays of light are united as one, in a similar way that the entire spiritual hierarchy is united as one soul, namely the Creator. 'Ray of Light' is a title for a specific or focused consciousness of the Creator, like a feeling or comprehension. This consciousness or wisdom is cocooned within energy which manifests as light and colour.

Each ray or aspect of the Creator's consciousness can trigger different emotions, actions and experiences within our physical lives. How we perceive the consciousness held within the rays of light and their colours depends on our present and past experiences and general level of growth; the level of awareness we have gained by evaluating all past lifetimes. To embody all twelve rays of light is our current mission, understanding their meaning in our individual realities by interpreting the rays of light as we experience and use them in our daily lives.

In the past we have been told to anchor and invoke the rays of light into our beings, but now as we evolve, a new appreciation of the rays and their purpose is coming forth; the rays are actually schools of spiritual learning helping us to understand the Creator, ourselves, our souls and abilities beyond our physical bodies.

All of the twelve rays of light hold ashrams or special places of residence in the inner planes; they resemble vast schools of spiritual learning and discovery. By connecting, understanding and integrating with each ray of light and visiting the ashrams of the rays, we can enrol ourselves in a special spiritual school that will accelerate us to achieve mastery, ascension and a new absolute aspect of the Creator within us.

The twelve rays of light originate from the core of the Creator's soul. At this vibration they are clear and invisible light, as their qualities are of the purest love although their focus remains the same. The twelve rays of light exist at each level or department in our universe. At a planetary level we experience the lowest vibration of these twelve rays of light; this is why their colours are so vibrant and pronounced. As we evolve beyond the planetary twelve rays of light, we will anchor the solar level twelve rays of light into our beings which are of a slightly higher vibration, suggesting their speed of vibration is quicker. We will also discover new rays of light and colours that hold different qualities and expressions of the Creator's soul, appropriate to our growth at the solar level.

These twelve rays of light available to us now will constantly be a part of our spiritual growth, whether we exist at a solar level or the highest of all, a cosmic level. It is for this reason that we must focus our energies and concentration on integrating, accepting and discovering the rays of light while we are on the Earth, as they are our spiritual tools of life and growth through the spiritual hierarchy, remaining within our souls at many different vibrations. It is because of the importance of the rays of light within the spiritual hierarchy that many Ascended Masters work as Chohans or within the ray ashrams on the inner planes of the spiritual world; the twelve rays are tools of spiritual growth for every soul, whether they exist in a physical or light body.

Many of us on the Earth express the qualities of certain rays of light without even realising it. The twelve rays of light are already a part of our souls, we have just yet to understand that everything we need and desire is within our souls waiting to emerge. To evolve spiritually we must become aware of the rays that we naturally anchor into our beings and realities, while understanding the rays that will most benefit our development. When we understand and use the rays of light in our lives, we create balance within our energy systems and embody a greater unity with the Creator.

Awareness and understanding of the rays with a conscious effort to invoke them into our lives is the key to working with these twelve spiritual schools of light. There is a need for humanity as individuals and as a whole to draw on the correct rays to assist their lives, their own inner as well as planetary peace, and the ascension process on the Earth. By understanding and using the rays we can transform our lives. With the aid of the Creator's energy we can achieve the goals and plans that our souls created for our current embodiment on the Earth as a form of guidance to ensure ascension is achieved.

We are not alone when faced with the mission of understanding and integrating the twelve rays of light, as there are Chohans, with teams of many different Masters and Angels working within each ray ashram that can be contacted and that will assist us in our mission of discovering and becoming united with the Creator's divine expressions and qualities. When we know the name of the Ascended Master or team members governing a certain ray, and their focal expressions or qualities, it is easier for us to invoke their assistance in our lives.

We need to consider that each ray of light has different vibrations of the same energy: there is a lower and a higher aspect of the Creator's loving expressions. People who are unaware of the concept of the rays of light naturally anchor the lowest form of energy from each ray. But when we actively invoke the rays of light to intertwine into our lives, we must remember to invoke the highest vibration available to us from each ray. This will ensure we gain the correct energy vibration for our growth processes without the energy being so high that it harms our physical body or so low that its effects are minimal. It is due to the many levels of vibration within one planetary ray of light that we can interpret the rays of light as different and diverse colours and shades of light.

The rays of light are anchored into our lives and beings in so many different ways; our physical, mental, emotional and spiritual bodies, as well as our soul and monad each anchor a different ray of light, demonstrating the different levels and aspects of our growth process.

Even our chakra systems are connected with the twelve rays of light. However, the colours of the rays and the colours of the chakras do not always marry; we must understand that the twelve rays of light in their purest form are clear so our chakras can hold their known colours while anchoring a certain ray of light that may be of a different colour.

For example, our root chakra at the base of our spine is usually of a red colour. This doesn't always mean that the first ray of light, which may also be seen as a red colour, is anchored into the root chakra; it all depends on the individual's spiritual growth process and the level of awakening or realisation they have obtained. The rays that the physical, mental, emotional and spiritual bodies – as well as the chakras anchor can change as we progress up the spiritual ladder, securing greater light into our beings.

Until recently it was improbable that our soul would change the ray of light that it anchors, as the soul chooses a ray that expresses and encourages its purpose or mission on the Earth before its embodiment. In our modern day time is quickening, and people are accelerating at a speedy pace, which means that the soul can switch to a different ray of light if a major growth process has occurred and the ray that was originally anchored no longer holds its purpose.

As our soul begins to present different rays of light to us at different stages of our growth we begin to realise that the ultimate goal of our soul is to hold and emanate all rays of light simultaneously, as this would signify a complete integration with the Creator's soul at a planetary level or higher levels of the spiritual hierarchy. The goals of the other aspects of our body are identical. By discovering the ray that our souls have anchored for our current lifetime or at different stages of our growth, we can comprehend and appreciate the energy, divine qualities and maybe even the purpose of our soul on the Earth.

For example, if the soul anchors the second ray into its being then it is very likely that experiencing and expressing pure love and a focus on spiritual education, learning or teaching would be the goals of the soul while on the Earth. It is not essential to understand the different rays that the many aspects of our beings connect with, but it is vital we follow our inner guidance and gut feelings when we feel an attraction, familiarity or resonance with a certain ray or rays of light. The desire to connect with a certain ray usually symbolises the need for that ray's energy and qualities in the individual's life in order to create balance or to develop greater skills from within.

Even countries, mountains, cities, towns and houses anchor one or two of the twelve rays of light into their energy and atmosphere, to support or nurture the people living within and around the area. We are all influenced by the twelve rays of light in so many ways that they can cause an imbalance in our bodies and energy systems; this is because we cannot as yet appreciate the expansiveness of our beings and how all the twelve rays are united as one within our beings, on the Earth and throughout the universe.

As we naturally anchor positive aspects of the rays into our beings, we can also attract negative aspects of the rays by our negative thought patterns, judgments and actions. The rays that are anchored into our cities, towns, houses or communities are created or attracted by the thought process or actions of the majority of people in that area. It is our mission and duty to take control of our beings and surroundings in a loving way, ensuring we invoke the necessary rays to assist us rather than leaving it to chance as to which ray of light we receive as an individual and as a community. Without focus we always receive the lowest aspect of any ray of light, but with conscious action and a positive thought process we can transform our planet and civilisation into a peaceful, balanced and harmonious haven within which to exist and learn, where all twelve rays of light are anchored equally or as needed into the Earth and united as one in every soul.

To invoke the energy and presence of a certain ray of light into our lives and beings, we need only address the Chohan or the quality of the ray, explaining that we would like to receive the perfect amount of energy for our growth process, asking for his or her assistance and the influence of the ray in our lives. When we have gathered even a small amount of knowledge about each ray, this aids us in creating our own affirmations that express our creativity and resonate with our being and growth. We are permitted to ask on behalf of our community, town, city or country. Here is a sample invocation you could use to connect with one of the twelve rays of light. You can create a similar invocation to anchor light into a place that needs assistance:

'Protected and guided by my angels and spirit guides, I invoke the energy, wisdom and positive qualities of the (Number) ray of light to flow through every aspect of my being and to assist me in my life today. I invoke the Chohan of this ray (Name) to oversee the light entering into my being, ensuring I absorb the perfect amount and intensity to assist me in my current spiritual

growth process on the Earth. Allow me to understand the qualities and in-fluences of this ray so I may integrate its energy deeper within my being. Thank you.'

When we invoke any of the twelve rays of light we must under-stand that this light can be expressed to us in many ways by the Masters of the rays. They can send a beam of light into our beings, surround us in a musical tone or vibration that symbolises the ray, or they can even place a word or symbol within our aura representing the ray of light, to attract the energy we desire into our beings. The way in which we receive the energy of the rays depends on our receptivity; the Masters have to discover what we respond to with the greatest results. A tone or musical note when performed near us may create the best impact on our energy systems, even if we cannot physically hear the sound; we will feel its sensations within our auras and bodies. In order to fully accept the light, vibrations and qualities of the rays, we should ensure we are open to receiving the energy in any form. When we remove limitations and restrictions created by the mind, we receive a greater concentration of energy from the twelve rays of light. If we are fortunate we may even obtain from the Chohans of the rays the special tones or symbols for each ray to allow us to use them in our lives as keys to unlocking the energy and wisdom of the twelve rays of light.

It is the first three rays of light that are classed as the foremost energies or rays of the Creator's soul; this is because of their power and great influence on our Earth and in the spiritual hierarchy. If we only accept and understand the teachings of these first three rays, we will accelerate dramatically along our spiritual path. The three rays of light are classed as key rays because they were the first to be introduced to the Earth and humanity.

The next four rays of light are understood as extensions of the third ray of light, mainly because the third ray supports their qualities and expressions of the Creator's energy, helping them to manifest in an acceptable way for us to absorb their energy. We need to focus on integrating and accepting the teachings of the first seven rays of light, as they present to us a solid and thorough spiritual awakening and awareness process, in preparation for anchoring the remaining five rays of light. The five latter rays of light are known as the higher rays because of their association with advanced spiritual practices, working towards the development of the soul. The twelve rays of light together lead us through a unique ascension and expansion course, allowing us to evolve to new levels of consciousness. All rays of light are equal; their focus is just positioned on different aspects of our souls and spiritual growth process.

We must remember that we all link into the rays of light in a unique manner, therefore we view the rays of light in diverse ways. The rays can appear differently to people in separate areas of the Earth because the vibration of their soul, country and the atmosphere around them will influence their experience of the rays' energy and consciousness. As we consider numerous people on the Earth linking into the same rays of light, we may realise it is akin to each person travelling into a country from a different direction, each one representing a new access, perspective and understanding.

It is important to be respectful to all information brought forth concerning the rays, as through greater comprehension we begin to understand their truth. In fact, the colours and chohans of the rays are not significant; it is our acceptance of the qualities and consciousness of the rays that is crucial to our unification with the Creator. The understanding that I have accepted through my channel, perspective and connection with the Creator is now explained as a means to aid your own unique integration, exploration and comprehension of the rays of light, qualities, consciousness and expression that extend from the Creator's soul. Remember that our ultimate goal is to hold all twelve rays of light – or twelve manifestations of the Creator – within us, actively using and demonstrating them in every aspect of our reality on the Earth.

Let us now awaken to the support and wisdom we can gain from the spiritual hierarchy through this process of anchoring the twelve planetary rays of light into our beings and realities on the Earth.

CHAPTER 15

MASTER EL MORYA AND
THE FIRST RAY OF LIGHT

Master El Morya is an Ascended Master from the Earth school. He lived as Abraham, father of the Jewish race, and as one of the three wise men who travelled to the birth of Jesus. Like most Ascended Masters he has overcome the initiations and lessons of Earth school and now occupies an important role in the spiritual hierarchy. Master El Morya is the Manu Allah Gobi's assistant. This may sound as if his responsibilities are minor, but as with all the Masters connected with the rays, his work is immeasurable. The Manu delegates much of his work to Master El Morya, and is also training him to become the next Manu once Allah Gobi evolves to a new position.

Master El Morya assists the Manu in his work with the spiritual and Earth governments, as well as understanding and distributing the will and plans sent by the Creator through the hierarchy. Let us not forget that while Master El Morya is working with the Manu and the other Masters of the rays, his focus is also placed on his own spiritual progression, and of course governing the first ray of light. Master El Morya holds the title of Chohan or governor of the first of the main three rays of light.

The first ray is of a red colour and holds the divine qualities of the Creator's will within its energy, to be invoked and absorbed both by us, and the Masters on the spiritual planes. At a lower level the red energy of the first ray can offer courage, confidence, determination, strength, bravery, action, boldness and focus. This fiery energy helps many souls on the Earth to achieve their goals and gives them the qualities that are needed to overcome challenges and lessons. Without the first ray of light we would not have the energy, power or driving force to stimulate us to follow our spiritual path with passion.

Whenever we feel lazy with lack of energy, we can invoke the first ray of light to charge us with the perfect amount of energy to lift our spirits and assist us in becoming active in our lives. The red ray of light is a powerful energy and when invoking it we must always call on the guidance of Master El Morya, ensuring that we state we wish to receive the perfect amount of this red energy for our beings and growth. Receiving too much energy from this ray could cause an imbalance. But we mustn't be fearful when using the ray as it is vitally important for our growth. We must trust we will always receive the perfect amount of energy for our beings and journeys on the Earth.

Depending on their jobs, personalities and missions, some people will draw on the first ray of light more than others, but our mission is to integrate specifically the first three rays of light into our beings in a harmonious fashion that aids our growth. As we become more involved with the first ray of light and delve deeper into its levels of energy, we understand that it holds and promotes straightforward-ness, fearlessness and accomplishment – qualities greatly needed in all light beings and souls on the Earth following a spiritual path. The more we understand about this ray, the more we realise it is not only an intense and powerful fiery energy, but it holds the will, desires and wishes of the Creator for humanity, the Earth and universe as well as our individual souls. The plans of the Creator exist within the first ray of light for all on the spiritual planes to access, understand and use to play their part in manifesting the Creator's will at a planetary level.

Many of us follow the wisdom of guides who push us along certain paths. Our guides are following the wisdom of our souls, but also abide by the will of the Creator. The guidance we are given not only nurtures our souls but produces actions that assist numerous people in their growth. Each of us is involved in the divine plan and will of the Creator on the Earth, but most of us are unable to understand this or distinguish the divine plan within the options given by our minds and souls. We have free will on the Earth and therefore have the choice of which path we should take in our lives, but when we devote our lives to the Creator, we are guided by the hand of the Creator and the spiritual hierarchy to act out the will of the Creator for the evolution and development of humanity.

Our choices affect many; sometimes more people than we are aware of. When synchronicities appear in our lives, small or large, it is a symbol from the Creator that we are following the correct path, following the guidance of our souls, and are integrating the divine plan into our realities. It is impossible for us currently to comprehend the will and purpose of the Creator, but we can have courage in the inspiration within us, taking action when it is needed. Through our actions we contribute to the intentions of the Creator. Integrating with the divine plans of the Creator will allow us always to be in the correct place and time to receive divine intervention.

Master El Morya teaches us the desire to accept our own inner power, to love others as we love ourselves, to crave and digest valued information, to harmonise with everything and everyone since we are the Creator manifested in all forms. He enhances within us the desire to act out the will of the Creator and stand as the Creator on the Earth, to help one another and to express the sacred energy within our souls fearlessly. Master El Morya offers those on the spiritual path the willpower to achieve these wonderful goals so we may integrate the Christ and the Active Intelligence of the Mahachohan into our beings, opening our hearts to Lord Buddha for guidance and encouragement, and to receive the planetary white consciousness of light. We are then able to step closer to becoming united with the wondrous energy of the Creator.

Master El Morya is a Master of love and light, embodying the energies of the Creator. He uses this life force to access and anchor the will of the Creator and the red ray into the Manu ashram, into the ashram of the first ray of light, into the twelve rays of light on the inner planes, and into the Earth.

Master El Morya is supported in the ashram of the first ray by many Masters and light beings working with the students that visit the ashram in their light bodies from the Earth and throughout the universe. There are Masters whose mission is simply to channel the red ray of light to those who invoke it on the Earth and to people, places, companies and regions that Master El Morya and the Manu have determined as specifically needing their light. Other Masters work with the kingdoms, realms and dimensions on the Earth and in the universe to integrate the will of the Creator into all.

Archangel Michael and his female aspect Archangel Faith assist Master El Morya and stand as powerful figures of protection. A deep connection can be found between the first ray of light and the Angelic and Elemental Kingdoms, as all are assisting the Creator in developing the evolution of humankind. Those of the Fairy Kingdom receive the will of the Creator and their instructions to oversee the Earth from the first ray Masters, as do the Angelic Kingdom. I don't think we can even begin to imagine how interconnected every part of the spiritual hierarchy is or the important role that we play within it.

The ashram of the first ray of light is open to visitors from the Earth; you can meet with the Masters for greater understanding and information about the ray by asking before you fall asleep at night to be taken by your guides to the first ray ashram while your body rests.

To connect with the first ray of light, invoke the Master El Morya and his assistants to anchor the perfect amount of positive and high vibrational energy for you into your being from the red ray ashram. The energy will flow into your physical body and aura through your crown chakra at the top of your head, flowing down your energy systems and into the Earth. Visualising or accepting the energy during meditation will allow an integration to occur. You can invoke the first ray of light during your daily routine when you need a boost or extra courage. Ask and you will receive.

The first ray of light can assist you if you feel as though you have lost your way on your physical or spiritual paths, or need new challenges or direction in your life. You can invoke Master El Morya to clear all confusion, leading you forth to create new connections that are needed or that you may have been searching for to continue your growth. Divine guidance and inspiration come to you in many forms. To instigate this process, invoke and absorb the red ray of light and Master El Morya's guidance into your heart and soul. He will anchor the divine plan and will of the Creator into your being and reality so that it may unfold before you. Allow yourself to experience the marvellous and awe-inspiring, powerful energy that emanates from Master El Morya and the first ray of light.

CHAPTER 16

MASTER JOSHUA AND
THE SECOND RAY OF LIGHT

The second ray of light, which is headed by Lord Maitreya, is of a blue colour and holds the Creator's qualities and expressions of love and wisdom. It is a pure ray that touches the hearts of the drowsy souls on the Earth and awakens them with love to the light of the Creator and their soul's manifestation on the Earth. The role of the second ray of light is to spread love and wisdom to all on the Earth, supporting every soul in their quest for spiritual enlightenment.

Love is the essence of the Creator's soul. It is in manifestation as the Christ Consciousness and is present within every particle of energy in the spiritual hierarchy. The energy of love can appear as pink, golden, green or blue colours, but in truth love is present within all colours, rays and energy vibrations. It is the bond that unites every energy and soul together. Without love we would experience separation. Love is the almighty power of the Creator, it is transformational, inspirational, healing, nurturing, and when embodied can unite us with the Creator, our inner souls and the truth. All qualities of the Creator and twelve rays of light stem from the loving core of the Creator. By embodying love we learn to love ourselves unconditionally, dissolve separation, accept the energy of the Creator in its entirety and honour ourselves as magnificent beings of light.

Wisdom is the result of embodying, anchoring and expressing love. As we exist as the love of Creator on the Earth, we anchor the enlightenment and wisdom of the Creator into our minds, expanding our comprehension beyond limitations. The wisdom that emerges from the core of love enhances our spiritual development for the greater good for humankind. Wisdom unsupported by love can cause harm and destruction, and lead us from the path of the Creator. This is the reason that love is so prominently placed beside the teachings that inspire wisdom. When we truly embody wisdom we have expanded our awareness and comprehension beyond physical limitations of the mind and have anchored the energies of the

Creator's universe into our beings. Wisdom is the product of love, illumination and a rise in energy vibration. We may study with the Masters to instigate enlightenment, but the wisdom we hunger to understand is within our souls.

The love and wisdom energies of the second ray of light act as a support network for all light workers and hold the beacon of light to lead forth the light souls on the Earth. It is the second ray of light that is needed on the Earth now to inspire peace, love and tranquillity amongst humanity. We are taught by the second ray of light to love everything and everyone with all our hearts and souls, while searching for the wisdom stored within us, acting as loving expressions of wisdom who appreciate the loving wisdom of others.

This educational and supportive ray of light aids us in discovering and understanding the love of the Creator while realising its manifestation within our souls. Each of us has a soul or beacon of light that exists within our physical bodies. Some people have anchored their soul into their physical being, while others have yet to realise the light within them; even so a soul is present in some form within every physical body on the Earth. Our soul is our powerhouse; it is our essence and the truth of our beings. It projects love continuously, thus making it extremely receptive to the second ray of light. The soul is akin to a vast kingdom in itself, holding immeasurable amounts of wisdom and information that we cannot yet comprehend. The soul is an inner sanctuary from the physical world that we can connect with, integrating desired energies and qualities into our realities. Our souls store every experience and droplet of enlightenment we have absorbed in our past lifetimes on the Earth and in the spiritual hierarchy. Everything we desire and require to follow our spiritual paths successfully is hidden within our souls. In truth, we already have and understand what we seek, we just have to learn how to release it.

The mission of the second ray and its Masters is to unlock the divine within, through love and spiritual education. We may call on the second ray of light to aid us in activating, realising, integrating and, most importantly, understanding how to use our souls as tools for our growth and development. We may call on the second ray of light to increase the amount of love within our body by pouring the blue light of the ray into our beings.

Calling on the second ray for guidance in any aspect of our lives is also encouraged. Everyone on the Earth needs to experience love and unity with the Creator and their soul, so it is important for us to connect with this special ray of light. We must all adopt as our mission the focus of embodying the second ray of light in our actions, thoughts, emotions and realities so that love pours from us at every moment of the day. Even when we sleep we must aim to radiate love from our hearts and souls, by asking to exist as radiant beacons while we rest. For many light workers on the Earth it is this ray they feel the deepest connection with, as it holds the wisdom they wish to discover and aids them in enhancing the love within their bodies and lives.

The Masters of the second ray are consequently known as spiritual teachers for humankind, since out of the three rays they work the closest with humanity to develop the growth of love within the physical body. The second ray ashram is akin to a spiritual school, tutoring in a vast number of subjects and teachings connected to the energy of love. They run a spiritual school like no other on the second ray of light, aiding us in integrating the love of the Creator into our beings, while offering us light particles of enlightenment to restore our inner wisdom.

There is an extension to this ray known as the Synthesis Ashram. It is a wondrous place that is the focal point for many students from the Earth, who visit in their sleep states. The students come from far to learn how to merge the energy of the Creator with their physical body, to achieve integration with the rays, as well as understanding as to how to integrate the cosmic energies and higher aspects of their soul with their physical personality on the Earth.

The Synthesis Ashram uses the energy of the second ray of light to assist its students in achieving these practices; it also takes some of the workload from the second ray Masters. The Synthesis Ashram resembles a smaller version of the Christ Ashram and assists many souls in connecting with the Christ Consciousness energy. To enrol in the course within the Synthesis Ashram to integrate the energy of the second ray and the Christ consciousness, simply invoke the energy of the second ray to anchor into your being while expressing your wishes, allowing the Synthesis Ashram energies to flow through you. To complement this request and the teaching of the Synthesis Ashram, it is advisable to ask to visit the Synthesis Ashram during your sleep state or meditation. There is a strong connection between the second ray of light, the Christ Ashram, and the World Teacher Ashram, as both have similar missions.

The second ray ashram on the inner planes is currently experiencing a huge amount of change, and has been for some time. The previous Chohans of the second ray of light and Synthesis Ashram, Master Kuthumi and Master Djwhal Khul, continue to keep a close eye on the second ray ashram because of the vast volumes of souls gathering in this sacred place of learning, growth and integration. It is Master Joshua who currently takes the role of Chohan or overseer of the second ray and the Synthesis Ashram, with a vast team of co-workers.

Master Joshua acquired the role of Chohan of the Synthesis Ashram from Master Djwhal Khul. This occurred while Master Joshua was still in manifestation on the Earth as Dr Joshua David Stone. He anchored the energy of Synthesis Ashram into the Earth with Djwhal Khul, assisting in the running of the ashram on the inner planes. Master Joshua returned to the spiritual planes in 2005 to continue his role of governing the Synthesis Ashram. He was a wise and illuminated being on the Earth, who assisted a vast number of souls in awakening to the light and beginning their paths of ascension. He was a key figure in ascension, offering much guidance and examples of spiritual growth through his numerous books and lectures. His achievements were great and he still remains one of the most respected and trusted leaders of the ascension movement on the Earth at this time. He assists even more people now from the spiritual planes and continues to devote himself to the Earth and the evolution of humankind. Master Joshua works extensively with the Christ Lord Maitreya, as the Christ is training Master Joshua to replace him in the Christ Ashram if the time manifests.

Several Masters are being trained to occupy eventually the roles of Chohan of both departments within this ray. It appears that Master Joshua is performing the work of two Masters, but because of the connection that humankind is now building with the second ray of light, there is not just one Master leading the ray of light but a team of wise and loving Chohans whose names may not be known to the Earth. Master Joshua is the team leader, the person to whom the co-workers turn for guidance and training because of his direct connection and link with the Christ, Lord Maitreya, who is delegating the guidance of Lord Buddha.

There appear to be many Masters passing through the second ray ashram at an accelerated rate to follow other paths inside and outside the universe. It is the volume of people evolving and awakening on the Earth that is causing a mass gathering on the second ray of light. This is a wonderful image to envisage as it symbolises that the world as we know it is finally stepping up to the mark, following the guidance and wisdom of their souls. It is difficult to imagine how the second ray of light will appear in a few years' time when many souls who exist in a drowsy state on the Earth awaken to the light.

It is important to stress that the work of the second ray of light is still accurate and precise; it remains a peaceful heaven of love where wisdom can be explored and developed. This will never change because the purity of love entering and emanating from this ashram is magnificent. Don't refrain from visiting the second ray ashram or the Synthesis Ashram if you feel a connection with this ray of light or its Masters. Follow your intuition and anchor this blue light into your being during meditation and during your daily life. If you are ever unsure of the ray that is appropriate for you to invoke at certain stages of your growth, the second ray is always a good option as it offers valuable guidance and anchors love which can resolve all problems or situations in your life. Master Joshua and the resident Masters of the second ray of light have time to assist and work with every person on the Earth personally when you call on their energy or when you visit the ashram during your sleep state. It is an important place to visit for accelerated growth and support. It is the most magnificent way of connecting with the love of the Creator.

The simplest practice to experience the second ray of light and its divine qualities is to invoke the blue ray of light from the second ray ashram to channel into your body, entering through your crown chakra, continuing down your chakra column and into the Earth. Allow the blue energy of love and wisdom to merge into your body, aura and every aspect of your being. You can practise this either during meditation or when you have a quiet moment. It is advisable to call on Master Joshua to oversee this process, ensuring you receive the perfect amount of energy for your being and level of growth.

When you visit the second ray of light during meditation or your sleep state by simply asking, you will be greeted by many Masters that may be unknown to the Earth but are deeply respected in the spiritual hierarchy. You will have the opportunity to join group lectures lead by Master Joshua and the Masters of the second ray, with the chance to speak with other students visiting at the same time as you. Don't be disappointed if you don't remember your visits, but know the Masters still assist you when you are on the Earth. You can call on them to continue to anchor and integrate the second ray of light into your being. To integrate with the second ray of light is to integrate with the Creator's love.

The presence of Master Joshua, a figure of ascension, on the second ray symbolises the immense influence of the second ray of light in the Earth's current spiritual education and ascension. The fact that many wise and caring Masters are working as a team, equally sharing the responsibilities and leadership of the second ray ashram, is a sign to us of how we can achieve unity with the people in our lives, our communities, countries, and of course the Creator. The ego is eliminated from the equation and the souls of the Masters unite in the love and devotion they share for their work and mission on our behalf.

Archangel Jophiel and Archangel Christine are the chief angelic energies supporting and distributing the love and wisdom of the second ray. We can call on their combined presence to assist us in anchoring and integrating the second ray of light and its divine qualities into our beings. They will assist us in gaining further enlightenment concerning the ray and can even be invoked to transport us to the second ray ashram during our sleep state. The angelic love these two Archangels channel from the second ray into our beings, if we ask them to, is transformational and breathtaking.

It is important to mention that Master Joshua is an example of how we all can evolve and ascend from the Earth when we focus our minds, following the intuition of our souls and guides with a passion to embody the Creator's will, love and teachings. Master Joshua demonstrated and answered many questions for humankind while on the Earth and continues to do so now in the spiritual hierarchy.

CHAPTER 17

MASTER SERAPIS BEY AND
THE THIRD RAY OF LIGHT

Master Serapis Bey currently governs the third of the three main rays, which is under the directorship of the Mahachohan Saint Germain. He previously governed the fourth ray of light, which is an extension of the third ray, but as Paul the Venetian stepped forward to take on the role of Chohan for the fourth ray, Master Serapis Bey was allowed to move to his new position of working closely with the Mahachohan Saint Germain. Both have worked together in the past and hold a deep friendship. They have wise, illumined minds that are fitting for their work on the third ray of light.

The third ray of light is of a yellow colour holding the Creator's qualities and expressions of Active Intelligence relating to the effective focused thoughts of the mind. The yellow ray illuminates the mind with its vibrant colour, removing any unwanted or negative thought patterns that may taint its healthy function. Master Serapis Bey and Mahachohan Saint Germain see the mind as an important tool of the physical body and the soul. It is not only a means whereby we make decisions about our lives and paths, attaining wisdom offered to us due to our awakening, or even creating a correct plan of action; the mind is also a tool of manifestation and expansion.

In truth, the title of Active Intelligence means manifestation with the highest state of awareness. When a person has not awoken to the light of their soul their mind follows the guidance and controlling attitudes of the ego. It works on autopilot without a care for what it is creating. The lack of power from the soul means the person may only manifest small situations or fears into their life because of the ingrained attitudes and beliefs of society.

When a person awakens to their soul, the power within them and the love of the Creator, it is as though a new part of the mind is activated; the intellectual left side of the brain and creative right side of the brain are married to enhance the manifestation skills of the mind. To become truly intellectual one must grasp the physical and spiritual understandings of the Earth and spiritual planes, tying in the will of the Creator and the creative qualities of their soul.

This may be a difficult task on the Earth as false information weaves through life, but wisdom and intelligence can be extracted from the soul, as the soul holds everything we desire to understand and more. With the power and light of the soul running through and into the mind, the ability to manifest what we desire or the truth of the Creator, rather than our fears, becomes apparent. Of course, the mind must be focused and programmed with positive thought forms and affirmations, but each positive thought enhances the power of the soul, thus assisting the mind to manifest the thoughts that hold the most amounts of energy and life force.

The manifestation process could be compared to housing a rocket within your mind. All the positive thoughts of the same nature or subject enter into the rocket until there is no more space available. The soul is the fuel that ignites the rocket. If there isn't a significant amount of fuel or power to accelerate the rocket then it may not reach the source of the Creator. The positive thoughts then have no influence in physical life. If the love and passion of the soul is directed to the positive thoughts created in the mind then anything is achievable. This is the definition of Active Intelligence, actively using the mind to manifest the experiences, lessons, situations, dreams and desires of the soul.

Master Serapis Bey works with many beings on the Earth and through the universe, assisting them in mastering the mind and manifesting their desires. The more advanced students he inspires and tutors in the art of manifesting the divine within the soul into reality, which is the beginning practices of a soul merge with the physical personality or the light body, depending on where the soul is in residence. He can help people to manifest money, health, careers, love and the dreams of the personality. Anything is possible because a thought is an orb of light.

The Earth is a thought form from the Creator. It is a giant manifestation of light moulded until it vibrates at a slow speed. When we are connecting into the slow vibrations of the physical plane the mind is disconnected from the soul and so the manifestations of the mind are not significant for the soul's light path. Focusing on creating our realities allows the mind to quicken in vibration and connects us with a higher vibration that will materialise our thoughts onto the

Earth in physical form. It is Master Serapis Bey's purpose to assist souls in anchoring their positive thoughts into a physical form. We could say Master Serapis Bey is a Master of creation, expressing the Creator's abilities to manifest and form the universe.

Master Serapis Bey works directly with the Chohans of the first and second rays to assist in manifesting the will and love of the Creator onto the Earth and into the spiritual hierarchy, while also educating the students of the first and second ray in manifestation. He distributes his tuition and manifestation techniques to all rays of light, his ray being tremendously important as it is the building material of the spiritual hierarchy and the Earth. Master Serapis Bey assists the Mahachohan in overseeing the rays four to seven as they are extensions of the third ray of light. He channels energy and support into each of these four rays so they may carry out their mission with great precision.

Master Serapis Bey assists the Mahachohan with his work of manifestation on a higher level, demonstrating and anchoring onto the Earth the will and plans of the Creator that concern the entire civilisation, such as major changes in consciousness stimulated by a boost of energy from all three rays directed through the third ray to the Earth. The Mahachohan's and Master Serapis Bey's work is now building as they try to stabilise and manifest the major change of consciousness towards which humankind is moving. They seek to encourage a mass awakening while also stabilising the energies of the Earth and humanity so the process doesn't accelerate too speedily. Their roles on behalf of Earth and its civilisation are growing with every minute.

It is beneficial to ask Master Serapis Bey to oversee the speed at which our spiritual growth accelerates, ensuring it is correct for our beings, allowing us to reach the pinnacle point of our spiritual growth process with perfect timing relating to the changes occurring on Earth. By the guidance of our souls, he will have the permission to help accelerate our spiritual growth process when we need to achieve our soul's mission on the Earth in perfect time. This may seem a strange request as we all have our own individual paths; but the fact that we are all united as one also influences our growth process. Master Serapis Bey will ensure we accelerate forward, tying synchronisations into our lives that aid and combine with the growth of others.

Not even the Ascended Masters grow alone, their growth always influences others. When we embody our souls, we are extensions of our monadic or soul group. The many soul extensions of one monad, whether they are on the Earth or are Ascended Masters, evolve and grow together at similar rates. Everyone and every soul is interconnected, no soul is abandoned or left behind, all evolve at equivalent rates, with some accelerating more than others towards their monadic groups and the Creator's expansive soul.

The third ray of light holds many ways and tools to assist people on a spiritual path. The yellow ray of light can be invoked to illuminate the mind, removing confusion of any kind to bring clarity. When invoked it can enhance intellect and assist in expanding the mind to grasp new ideas. A surge in intellect, especially spiritual understanding, will always manifest from love: everything that manifests from or through the third ray of light comes from the loving source of the Creator. The yellow ray only manifests positive loving situations; it is the fear in the human mind that manifests negative situations.

We can invoke Master Serapis Bey and the third ray of light to support and develop our positive thoughts, and to manifest them into our realities. We can ask the Master to assist us when reading, attending meetings or lectures, so we can gain a greater appreciation, absorbing information with clarity and a Christ Conscious mind. The Chohan will remove all negative thought habits and their implications in our lives, if we ask him to, and will assist in manifesting the mind of the Creator into every living soul on the Earth. He will also help us to discipline our mind in order to gain peace and stillness, especially during meditation.

Although this is Master Serapis Bey's mission, we must support it by invoking his energy to assist in bringing love and a clear vision to humankind. This will anchor his energy into the Earth. Master Serapis Bey will tutor us in connecting with our minds and guiding with love, he will help us to access and use a larger amount of our brains to develop and understand new skills from the soul. If asked, he will open the energy of our minds to allow the wisdom of the Masters to flow into our thoughts, allowing us to communicate with the spiritual planes. The mind is not a negative tool but a positive tool when governed by love and discipline.

In past lifetimes on the Earth, Master Serapis Bey incarnated into the civilisations of Atlantis and Ancient Egypt at their most evolved stages. During these times the people on the Earth not only understood the power of the mind but used it to build their lives around them. Think how long and how much effort it takes us to build houses on the Earth. Some of the Atlantean and Egyptian people had the power to manifest houses, temples and pyramids with the power of their thought forms and the love of their souls.

We believe we are advanced beings because of our technology, but it has taken a great deal of influence from many souls incarnate on the Earth over generations and much experimenting to achieve our current status. In spite of everything, not all countries benefit from the growth of technology. We build machines to help us live in comfort. Yet the greatest machine known to humankind is the mind, but we don't use it. We have been taught by controlling authorities to abide by the ideas and instructions of others, accepting programming of our minds, which hinders the spiritual aspect of our beings.

Negativity and fear exert such powerful programming that controls our lives and stops us from achieving the goals of our souls. Prevailing over the ego is one of the challenges we must overcome on the Earth, but the lessons of mastering fear and negativity have been enhanced by the egos of the authoritative figures who energise the fear existing within humanity. Eliminating the negativity and doubtful thoughts of the ego that run constantly through our minds, even when we are unaware of their presence, is a major step in mastering and accepting the Christ Consciousness into our beings. In order to remove some of our programming we can begin to connect with our souls, following our inner guidance and intuition, which places our power with our souls rather than the ego.

Master Serapis Bey wishes to remove these limitations that are placed on humankind and their minds from birth. He wishes to aid every soul to manifest his or her own realities with the love of the soul and the Creator as a source and guide. When we as physical beings open our energy systems to the light and love of the Creator it is so much easier for Master Serapis Bey to help us. If every soul on the Earth were to invoke his guidance, we would see an instant positive and peaceful transformation in the human mind.

Let us make the work of both of the Masters less demanding by invoking Master Serapis Bey to oversee our growth process and to release the limitations of the mind in a gradual process so we may awaken to the truth and the power existing within our minds. In asking him to help us dissolve confusion and adopt clarity and discipline, we can concentrate on what is important rather than allowing our mind to wander without purpose.

The Master's past lifetimes on the Earth in Atlantis and Egypt have equipped him for his current work of manifesting the Creator's qualities on the Earth once more. The return of Atlantis on the Earth is not meant literally but symbolises the anchoring and full manifestation of the first three rays of light onto the Earth, allowing every soul to embody the highest vibration of each ray in a physical form and remember their truth. With Master Serapis Bey's assistance we can achieve this manifestation.

By directly speaking with Master Serapis Bey, we can anchor the light of his soul and the third ray into our minds and hearts, allowing the yellow ray to run through our bodies. We can ask the Master to assist us with any of the matters spoken of above; he will be more than happy to intervene divinely in our lives. As with all the rays, we can visit the third ray of light ashram during meditation or our sleep state, and we can ask to sit in Master Serapis Bey's ascension activation seat in Luxor on the spiritual planes any time throughout the day on the Earth. His energy and the light of his ashram will surge through our bodies and energy systems assisting us with our growth. Master Serapis Bey is a wise and illumined being who offers his services and the energy of the third ray of light to all.

The angelic presence working with and channelling the energy of the third ray of light to humanity comprises Archangel Chamuel and Archangel Charity. Both are masters at illumining the mind and eliminating confusion, and will assist us in mastering our thoughts. They assist Master Serapis Bey by aiding us to absorb the enlightenment and techniques of the third ray of light and the entire planetary level.
'I am the creator in manifestation.'

CHAPTER 18

MASTER PAUL THE VENETIAN AND
THE FOURTH RAY OF LIGHT

The fourth ray of light is an extension of the third ray of light, as are all rays four to seven. Each of these rays is overseen by the Mahachohan Saint Germain, who offers his guidance as well as the instructions of Lord Buddha to the Chohans of the rays three to seven. Each ray is integrated with the third ray of light; this ray assists the other rays in manifesting their qualities while helping to anchor the divine plan of the Creator onto the Earth.

It is Paul the Venetian, or Paul from Venus, who governs the fourth ray of light, which is represented as a green colour of light. Paul the Venetian is so named in reference to his previous incarnations, but he is fondly known by many on the inner planes as Paul of Venus, the star from which he extends. Paul the Venetian also has an Ascended Master who closely assists him with his work, named Master or Saint Paul; there are many other Masters, light beings and Angels who assist this ray in manifesting its divine qualities onto the Earth and within every soul.

Paul the Venetian is particularly skilled in governing this ray of light due to his past incarnations on the Earth. His two most famous existences were as an artist named Paul Veronese and as the sculptor, painter and architect Michelangelo. His past lifetimes on the Earth prepared him in resonating with the Creator's qualities of the fourth ray of harmony, beauty, creativity and the arts. As you can see, there are many aspects to the fourth ray of light, but most are focused on developing the right side of the human brain to allow the creative energy within the soul to swell and emerge.

Paul the Venetian and the fourth ray support and encourage all the souls in their careers or hobbies in the field of art - not just the subjects associated with art, but drama, dancing, writing, music and singing; in truth, any form of expression of a creative nature. Paul the Venetian assists people connected to this field in achieving their dreams, when they ask this of him, but his priority is to channel the love of the

Creator and the energies of the first and second ray into creative souls so that it may appear in their expressions of an artistic nature. He achieves this with the assistance of the third ray of light to anchor the truth and energy of the Creator into the creative pieces, objects, paintings, scripts, lyrics and choreography of souls on the Earth, allowing them to be viewed and accepted by all. Paul the Venetian charges the light of the Creator and Lord Buddha into every person who desires to express him or herself creatively so they may embody the fourth ray of light and the divine energy.

Once a connection has been formed, the creative person continues to spread to humankind through their work the energy of the Creator, or messages of inspiration. Humans are sometimes unaware of the energy emanating from the work of others, and yet unknowingly it assists many in awakening to the light of the Creator; like an invisible force influencing their lives. Those who are particularly gifted, or feel as though their talent came from nowhere, usually have a deep connection with the fourth ray of light and have built this connection through many lifetimes. They have learnt to express their soul light and love in a certain way and continue to do so in their current lifetime. These talented and creative people act as beacons of light for the fourth ray of light on the Earth. It is Paul the Venetian's purpose to assist every person focusing on expressing themselves creatively to reveal their inner light and soul, thus raising the energy vibration of humanity in an invisible way.

We can invoke Paul the Venetian to assist us with any of our creative projects, hobbies, careers or dreams. We must ask him to help us find a divine path to follow our creative desires, teaching us to channel the love and light of the Creator into everything we do. Invoke the Chohan of the fourth ray to reveal the creativity of your soul; everyone is creative whether they believe it or not, because creativity is the love of the soul in manifestation.

Art in all forms is a manifestation of beauty on the Earth; though of course we all have our own opinions on the definition of beauty. Master Paul the Venetian assists many in creating beauty in their realities. We all love to exist within a beautiful physical reality, but it is the beauty within that is the focal point of Paul the Venetian's work with humanity. He assists us in creating beauty in our lives so it may inspire the beauty within us to emerge. Each of us is a beautiful being. Our souls are so radiant, vibrant and luminous that as physical beings we cannot even comprehend the beauty hidden within our physical bodies. With advanced understandings and the ability to manifest our thoughts, we can integrate the beauty of our souls into our physical bodies to transform our appearances. It is all a question of mastery.

When we allow the beauty or the inner light of our souls to emerge, we attract greater beauty into our lives and learn to see the beauty of the Creator in every person, animal, building and object that we view, regardless of the actions of the person or how the object affects us. We see beauty within everything because we accept and understand the beauty that is within our own being. We can invoke Paul the Venetian and the fourth ray of light to assist us in understanding and mastering this lesson.

The fourth ray of light, of a green colour, not only enhances creativity and beauty but focuses on harmony which could be described as peace, balance and unity. In Paul the Venetian's eyes the Creator's quality of harmony takes many forms. The Master anchors and manifests harmony on the Earth and within the physical body to create inner and outer peace: peace within civilisations and between the soul and the mind. Paul the Venetian lays a blanket of light containing harmony around the Earth so all may absorb his energy, integrating it into their lives. When inner harmony manifests, outer harmony and balance are found between people; harmony allows the mind to be clear and the Christ to anchor into the soul and onto the Earth. When harmony is achieved, one has combined the many elements of the Creator's energy to create balance and the soul's power to create a whole.

In order to achieve and accept the qualities of harmony, we must wipe away all the negative thoughts, emotions, energy and situations that occur to us in our daily lives on the Earth. We must clear any unwanted stagnant energy and heal our beings and every situation with light, allowing harmony to rush onto our paths. Sometimes humans are unable to see the lessons placed on their paths. They are suffocated by the effect of negative situations and are unable even to contemplate invoking the light of the Creator. It is on these occasions that Master Paul the Venetian assists in removing all negativity to replace the situation and the frame of mind of the person with harmony. Each of us can invoke greater amounts of harmonious energy from the green ray into our lives by asking Paul the Venetian to anchor and integrate the fourth ray of light within our physical and spiritual beings.

Sometimes a conflict or negative situation has to occur in order for a soul to accept the energy of harmony into their life. Harmony can be obtained through many circumstances, but by invoking the energy of harmony from the green ray throughout our spiritual growth processes, we allow our beings to be cleansed, healed and balanced, thus removing major conflicts of any kind from our lives and paths. We then allow the beauty and creativity of our souls to emerge and integrate into our physical realities and bodies on the Earth.

The Master invites us to invoke his energy and the energy of the fourth ray into our beings so we may manifest the creativity, beauty and harmony of our souls and the Creator onto the Earth. He is open to students visiting him and his team in their fourth ray ashram during their sleep state or meditation for greater learning and understanding of the subjects discussed. If you are in need of healing, this is a wonderful ashram to visit.

As a gift, Master Paul the Venetian offers to all the ability to invoke the purest form of music from his ashram. This music is of a high vibration and can appear as a choir of heavenly Angels when summoned. You may not be able to hear the divine music with your physical ears, but your soul will soar with bliss from the beauty of the high frequency music surrounding your body. You can invoke this heavenly music while you meditate to raise your energy vibration, or you can ask for the music of the fourth ray ashram to surround you while your body rests and sleeps at night.

A vast team of Masters works alongside the Chohan; such as Master John Lennon, who holds the light of peace for all of humanity to access, to reduce fear, violence and anger. Master John Lennon accessed the fourth ray of light while he existed on the Earth and his music assisted our planetary awakening. He now works in the fourth ray ashram with music and tones to raise the consciousness of the Earth and the spiritual hierarchy. There are many other Masters who are similar to Master John Lennon, devoting their energies and efforts to the ray of creativity.

The kind and gentle souls of Archangel Gabriel and Archangel Hope work as a masculine and feminine energy with the fourth ray of light, emanating its divine qualities to all. Archangel Gabriel is particularly gifted in breaking down boundaries so communication may flow, whether with a physical or spiritual being. He uses and channels the harmonious green energy as a soothing balm for all who invoke his presence. You may wish to invoke Archangel Gabriel and Archangel Hope to assist in anchoring the green ray of light from the fourth ray ashram into your being.

CHAPTER 19

MASTER HILARION AND
THE FIFTH RAY OF LIGHT

Master Hilarion is a blaze of orange energy; he embodies the high vibrational qualities of the fifth ray of light within his light body and emanates his light to anyone who calls his name. Master Hilarion is known to hold within his soul the truth of the Creator and the universe we exist within. He has been given many insights through working on the fifth ray of light, and is entrusted by the more evolved spiritual Masters with important decoding work in order to discover new ways of growth or new wisdom.

The fifth ray of light is of an orange colour and holds a divine expression of the Creator's mighty mind; it energises science in all forms. Master Hilarion uses the wisdom, will and divine plan of the Creator, developing it beyond limitations until new truths and under-standings are born. We must remember that the Chohans of the rays and the Ascended Masters are always learning as we are. Master Hilarion has a great team of scientifically minded Ascended Masters working in his ashram, who are more spiritually connected with the Creator than we would imagine.

On the Earth we draw on the intellect of the left brain for scientific research, which can leave little room for spiritual practices. Within these scientific minds there is a belief that everything must be proven and evidence must be gained in order to understand the truth. The practices and beliefs of a spiritual person may not be accepted because of poor verification.

The Masters on the fifth ray of light do not hold these limitations but open their hearts to the love of the Creator and use this energy to fuel their research and ideas. They are the most evolved scientists in the spiritual hierarchy at a planetary level. Some of them focus on research while others create and devise new ideas, tools and ways to accelerate the spiritual growth of light workers on the Earth. With every fragment of their work, they hold their focus on reuniting the soul extensions of the Creator existing on the Earth with the inner planes and the love and light source of the Creator. There is no need for this focus to be programmed into their minds as it is a part of their souls; they have a passion for assisting humankind in ascending and embodying light.

Master Hilarion and his scientific Masters hold the science of the soul within their ashram. They understand the soul energy of individuals and the mighty soul of the Creator, holding tools and practices to strengthen the power, love and intensity of each and every soul, whether they are on the Earth or the spiritual planes. Understanding the soul and how to enhance its presence is the central focus of the fifth ray of light, and can be understood fully when accepting the highest vibration of light in the fifth ray ashram.

There are many layers to the fifth ray ashram, as new Ascended Masters who wish to work on this ray enter the ashram, they begin with a position working with the lowest energy vibration. The work of the lower energies of the orange ray is still extremely important on the Earth; the Masters assist many scientists in their work covering all subject matters. The Masters working on the fifth ray are following a unique path of spiritual growth for their souls, moving through the levels of the ashram.

People with a career in science of any kind can invoke the orange ray to illuminate their mind, removing obstacles to allow them to discover the information they seek. The scientific Masters of the fifth ray anchor, where it is possible, the love and wisdom of the Creator into physical scientists and their work as a form of anchoring the energy of the Creator into the Earth. Doctors and surgeons all work with the lower energies of the fifth ray. In truth, anyone who is involved in solving problems, finding the truth or discovery draws on the orange ray without even realising. Through physical thoughts, ideas and experiments light is anchored onto the Earth. The orange ray tries to enlighten those who are receptive, by sharing new tools or equipment to develop the spiritual acceleration of humans, but there is also an influence from the dark side that focuses on the ego, invisibly controlling some minds to create weapons and machines that are not from the core mind and soul of the Creator. This is why the fifth ray is using the energy of the third ray to assist in manifesting the love and divine ideas of the Creator into the receptive scientific and intellectual minds on the Earth.

At the middle level of the orange energy within Master Hilarion's ashram are the ideas, concepts, tools and plans that could transform the world and the way we live our lives on the Earth. If the information at the middle level were accessed and, most importantly, understood by many people on the Earth, then they would be able to assist in creating peace on the Earth. They would solve all problems of famine, disease, poverty, pollution, including electro-magnetic pollution, global warming and war.

The solutions to these problems, which cause great suffering to humankind, have already been designed and are waiting to be accessed from the fifth ray of light. The scientific Masters hold the answers and solutions for all problems on the Earth, but it is currently difficult for humans to access them as they need to gain a greater awareness to understand the plans that are predominantly focused on the light of the Creator. There are many people and beings whose focus is on the dark side. These beings will do anything to stop the wisdom of Master Hilarion's ashram entering into the minds of humans on the Earth. Master Hilarion must always be aware and alert for the correct times to introduce new ideas onto the Earth. Of course, as humanity awakens to the cruelty on the Earth and becomes aware of the power existing within their souls, the wisdom within Master Hilarion's ashram will quickly spread onto the Earth to transform the lives of many.

At the highest possible vibration of the orange ray of light are the techniques, practices and discoveries connected to the science of the Creator's soul and soul extensions on the Earth and in the spiritual hierarchy. Within this level are the secrets of spiritual evolution and ways to comprehend and integrate the soul into a physical body or light body. The fifth ray of light holds every particle of information we hunger to discover, especially concerning the soul, making it a fascinating ashram to visit.

If you find the work of Master Hilarion resonates with you, if you are seeking divine inspiration for a scientific or a spiritual project, or you wish to begin to integrate your soul with your physical personality, then you may wish to invoke the energy of the orange ray to anchor into your being during meditation and throughout your day. Visiting the ashram in your sleep state or during meditation will allow you to connect on a deeper level with the fifth ray of light, the scientific Ascended Masters working on this ray and Master Hilarion.

You can ask your Angels to transport you to this ray safely, asking that you focus on expanding your mind to gain a greater understanding, or that you work with the higher vibrational Masters to begin to anchor and integrate your soul into your physical personality and reality. The Masters share advanced wisdom and technology that inspires soul integration.

When you enter into the ashram of the fifth ray you step into an energy space that is free from limitations, and it can be an awesome experience if you are lucky enough to remember it when you return to the Earth. Master Hilarion is available to be invoked and will assist you with your spiritual and physical paths, assisting in solving problems or confusion, inspiring you to discover the truth of the Creator in everything you do. If you are consulting a medical person or healer about health problems then you can ask the fifth ray of light to ensure the person you are consulting draws from the orange ray of light, anchoring the soul and truth of the Creator into their being and work, especially if they are performing a diagnosis or surgery on your body. This will ensure they work for your soul's greater mission on the Earth and channel light into your being, guided by the fifth ray Masters.

We can ask for the truth of the Creator to be anchored onto the Earth through the development of technology and science by the aid of the fifth ray of light. This is wonderful service to humanity as it will assist in removing unwanted developments that hinder the spiritual growth of souls.

Master Hilarion is a key figure of the fifth ray of light as he embodies, like a computer, all the wisdom and practices that are discovered and are worthy of maintaining. He is also a generous and loving character devoted to the Creator, emanating pure love. He connects and links his energy into the solar, galactic and universal levels within our spiritual hierarchy to raise the energy of his ashram and to fuel his mind, soul and ashram with greater understanding and enlightenment to aid the work of his team of Masters. He holds a great deal of power within his ashram, but the love of his soul counteracts any urges to abuse his power. We could learn from his loving example.

Master Hilarion is greatly respected for his work, the smooth running of his ashram and the abundance of ideas flowing from the orange light. This is why he also holds a position on the eighth dimension. The eighth dimension could be compared to a laboratory or chamber, experimenting with ideas and techniques to find solutions to problems. These inspirational ideas or projects come forth from the ninth dimension and its Masters.

Each dimension is a level of consciousness that will and can be experienced through spiritual growth and awakening. Working in this consciousness and space allows Master Hilarion and the Cosmic Masters to test ideas, techniques, and even cosmic energy waves to ensure they create the perfect acceleration for humankind. This laboratory is so advanced they can see the effects each idea will have on the Earth and its people without upsetting our lives on the Earth. If the results are unsatisfactory then the tests can be aborted while the successful plans are put into place on the Earth, sometimes entering through the fifth ray of light, using it as a tool to anchor the plan of the Creator onto the Earth.

Archangel Raphael and Archangel Mary work with the energy of the fifth ray of light because of its unique awakening practices and the truth of the Creator that is constantly being discovered in the ashram. Archangel Raphael and Archangel Mary assist Master Hilarion by anchoring the orange ray of light into receptive souls on the Earth to boost the influence of the divine within. They also oversee any new ideas or projects that are anchored onto the Earth, to ensure everything runs smoothly, reporting back to Master Hilarion any problems or interesting results that have occurred.

Archangel Raphael and Archangel Mary are powerful healers of humankind; this is because they anchor energy from the fifth ray of light into their beings, helping them to heal individuals from the inside out. They hold the most effective healing tools and skills because of their unique understanding of how the soul and the energy around our physical bodies work. This is why they are known as gifted Archangel healers.

We can invoke Archangel Raphael and Archangel Mary to aid our healing, empowering the influence of our souls in our realities, and to assist us in connecting, visiting and understanding the fifth ray of light.

Let us invoke Master Hilarion and his team of Masters to help us understand the soul, to integrate the light of the Creator into our beings and to ensure that the development of technology on the Earth is for the best possible outcome for our divine loving and spiritual souls. Allow Master Hilarion to lead you forth on a journey of discovery of the wisdom, power and skills existing within your soul.

Chapter 20

Master Lanto and the Sixth Ray of Light

Through the indigo ray of light that blazes from the sixth ray ashram, the presence of a small, ancient Chinese Master appears. From the core of his being an intense energy is shared with us, demonstrating Lord Lanto's passion for the Creator and an inner power that unmistakably originates from love. He is the pure embodiment of the indigo light and shines like a vibrant indigo star in the night sky.

Lord Lanto is a quiet, serene and tranquil Master; nothing can stir him from his meditative state of being, the deep bond and constant connection with the soul of the Creator. It is because of his profound dedication and devotion to the Creator and the Creator's soul extensions that Master Lanto has been appointed Chohan of the sixth ray of light. Master Lanto acquired his position some time ago after training with Master Sananda and Lady Nada in the role of a sixth ray Chohan. When the occasion came for Master Sananda to take his new position with Master Kuthumi as World Teacher, Master Lanto worked for a very short period with Lady Nada until she was ready to transfer to the eighth ray of light to become its Chohan. Master Lanto was then allowed to take sole control of the sixth ray of light, allowing him to truly integrate with the role and the divine qualities of the sixth ray.

Master Lanto previously existed within the second ray ashram, working very closely with the Chohan Master Kuthumi. He was accepted as a main and prominent teacher of the high vibrational light of the second ray; Master Kuthumi often delegated some of his responsibilities to Master Lanto so that he could develop, understand and assist students in integrating with the second ray of light. His wisdom was most respected within the second ray ashram and many students visited the ashram especially to seek guidance from him.

It was his last lifetime on the Earth that obtained him a position to work alongside Master Kuthumi in the second ray ashram. He was an ancient Chinese Master who developed the luminosity and power of his soul within his physical body so profoundly that his soul light shone through his skin, clearly evident for people on the Earth to view. In a previous lifetime Master Lanto was a disciple of Master Jesus; this is one of the reasons that Master Sananda selected him to become his successor for the sixth ray of light. It was also because of his sweet nature and constantly loving temperament. The devotion that Master Sananda poured into his role as Chohan, the energy of the Christ and the energy of the second ray, continue to influence the sixth ray of light through Master Lanto.

The devotional energy of the indigo ray is one of the purest forms of acceptance of the Creator's energy, existence, divine plan, intervention, love, wisdom and light. The indigo ray holds the deepest devotion for every aspect of the Creator within the spiritual hierarchy. Many Ascended Masters draw on this divine and inspirational energy to boost their own connections with the Creator.

As humans on the Earth, we can be devoted to or have a love of many things, hobbies or interests. We can even be devoted to our careers and family life. It is similar to an invisible bond expressing our love for situations, objects or people who inspire us. When we experience this devotional energy we are connecting with just a small percentage of the sixth ray of light – the lower aspects. Feelings of devotion are what tie us together, and also single us out if our interests are different from others. Devotion can be defined as an affection or attachment which we all understand and can relate to; it is a form of love.

On the higher levels of the indigo ray, devotion is defined as a deep connection, acceptance and oneness with the Creator; this is the truth of the sixth ray and the mission of Master Lanto. He wishes to assist light beings on the Earth in awakening to the light of the Creator, accepting the Creator's energy, realising that the divine source energy of the Creator exists within every manifestation on the Earth. Through these realisations we will develop a deep unwavering affection for the Creator and a feeling of unity.

Master Lanto works with the emotions, feelings and soul of the physical body or light body to assist the person in accentuating and understanding the quality of devotion. His energy is present in our realities and within our beings now, but in small amounts. To truly appreciate and attain the purest form of devotion, we must open our beings and souls to Master Lanto and allow him to create a flow of energy from the sixth ray ashram into our bodies, exiting into the

Earth. With the indigo energy running through our bodies we are able to become receptive to the energy of devotion with which Master Lanto works.

Devotion is not a controlling aspect, nor is it a power that drives us to achieve at any cost; devotion at its highest vibration is a unity with the Creator's soul. This is the focus of all souls on the Earth. It may be buried beneath the personality, but there is a glimmer of light within every person on the Earth, a wish to be connected and united with the Creator as a child wishes to be near its parents. When we develop this glimmer of light, it blossoms and manifests as our soul, enhancing within us a passion or necessity to connect with the Creator on deeper level. A devotion to the Creator is a need to love and to experience love of the purest form.

Alongside devotion, the sixth ray of light also expresses the truthfulness, discipline, purity and trust of the Creator. We can invoke the sixth ray of light for uplift when we are feeling down or low in energy and need support; it is especially valuable to invoke the indigo ray when we lose our faith in the Creator and ourselves through traumatic experiences or disappointments. Master Lanto can realign us with the Creator so we can receive and understand the love of the Creator once more. Embodying the highest energy of the sixth ray throughout the day with the intention to connect on a deeper level with the Creator can build or draw from the soul devotion and love that have never been apparent before.

In truth, devotion is a development of the soul. The soul unconditionally and permanently loves the Creator with all its might, but we as the physical personalities of the soul do not experience the same emotion and can sometimes doubt the Creator's existence until we allow our physical personality to integrate with our soul energy. Invoking, anchoring and embodying the indigo ray will assist with soul merges and integrations and will connect us with greater aspects of light, love and wisdom to heighten our faith.

While our focus is the energy of the Creator, we mustn't forget the manifestation of the Creator within our physical bodies. Master Lanto's mission is to assist the physical personality and mind in accepting the soul into its body and reality, devoting every moment of the day to the energy of the soul.

Our devotion firstly lies with our soul and then with the Creator, because we must accept ourselves as the Creator on the Earth. This is a major lesson to understand and one that Master Lanto is equipped to assist us with. The Chohan of the sixth ray asks us to devote every breath, thought and emotion to the development of our souls within our physical bodies. By following this practice we will accept the divine Creator within us, learning to honour, understand and become one with the mighty Creator while becoming one with our souls.

The sixth ray of light can act as a support network when we ask for its assistance, encouraging us to follow and accept the wisdom of our souls. To achieve this energy of support we can meditate and imagine that within every aspect of our beings is the energy of the indigo ray of light, descending into our beings through our crown chakras.

While we focus on devoting our every thought and action into anchoring the energy of the Creator into our beings, Master Lanto doesn't want us to give our power away to the Creator. He tutors us to love and accept the energy of the Creator into our lives with a mission to increase our faith, devotion and love with every step we take along our spiritual paths. To surrender to the energy of the Creator and the Creator's will in our lives is an aspect of the path of devotion, but we always hold responsibility over our own beings and actions. Surrendering will simply raise our vibrations so we may understand and grasp a new level of devotion that we can express to the Creator, receiving greater light.

To bathe in love and devotion of the purest form, ask Master Lanto to surround you in his energy or to transport you to his ashram during your sleep state. You will be cocooned in a deep love that can assist in accepting yourself as a worthy, precious and valuable jewel of light, learning to honour your true being, rather than your physical achieve-ments or personality. The energy of the indigo ray of light can assist you in accepting not just the Creator into your heart but the truth of your being.

The angelic presence of Archangel Uriel and Archangel Aurora assist Master Lanto in sharing the energy of the sixth ray with human-ity and the Masters on the inner planes at a planetary level. The energy of the sixth ray is an extremely sacred energy that all Archangels and Angels embody, but it is Archangel Uriel and Archangel Aurora who work alongside Master Lanto. Archangel Uriel is known as the wisest of Archangels. This is very interesting as he embodies the sixth ray of light completely, as well as all other eleven rays of light, but it appears that by completely integrating with the sixth ray energy Archangel

Uriel has evolved to become a radiant and knowledgeable messenger of the Creator. We can only wonder whether it is his sheer devotion that has allowed his soul to accept such vast and precious enlightenment.

We can invoke Archangel Uriel and Archangel Aurora to assist us in accepting the presence of the sixth ray within our beings and to help us to integrate it into our situations and realities on the Earth. They will assist us in holding our faith when experiences do not run as we originally planned. They can cradle us in their loving arms to ensure we retain our faith and connection with the Creator at all times.

Archangel Uriel is particularly skilful at sharing his wisdom and enlightenment with us to inspire us to accept and use the sixth ray of light, respecting its power and importance in our growth processes on the Earth. When we are confused we may call on Archangel Uriel to shower us in the sixth ray indigo light. When we have faith in ourselves, the Creator and our abilities, we are able to see the truth with clarity, integrating it into our minds and realities on the Earth.

Archangel Uriel and Archangel Aurora are renowned angelic teachers whom we can invoke to assist us in our development processes. It is important for us to understand that it is the sacred devotional energy of the sixth ray of light which is the supportive energy for all the teachings, inspirations and techniques they share with us to lead us forth along our spiritual paths. This comprehension should inspire us to invoke the sixth ray of light to become a constant energy and presence within every aspect of our lives on the Earth.

Let the indigo ray of light, Master Lanto, Archangel Uriel and Archangel Aurora assist you in experiencing the divine energy, happiness, bliss and love that encourage us to continue forth on our spiritual paths, to be united with the manifestation of the Creator within and around us. Let us accept this reality and integrate it into every moment of our lives so we can understand and feel the presence of the truthful and loving devotion of the sixth ray, our souls and the Creator while on the Earth.

CHAPTER 21

LADY PORTIA AND
THE SEVENTH RAY OF LIGHT

The seventh ray as of late has been subject to change, which can lead to some confusion as the time scale on the Earth is vastly different to the time periods on the inner planes. Time as we know it doesn't exist in the spiritual planes, and yet it is so prominent in our lives on the Earth; this can make it difficult for us to detect changes of roles within the spiritual hierarchy.

It is the Master Saint Germain who has for many years lovingly guided and governed the seventh ray of light which is of a violet colour. Master Saint Germain assisted many in understanding and using the violet flame of cleansing light to eliminate negativity of all kinds. It is because of the presence of the flame that the violet ray of light has become known as a transformational ray.

Working with Master Saint Germain during his time as Chohan was Lady Portia, who is a female aspect of the Master's soul. Lady Portia acted as the Master's assistant and embodied everything that Saint Germain discovered. As Master Saint Germain evolved to take the place of the Mahachohan, it is fitting that Lady Portia, an aspect of Saint Germain, became the new Chohan of the ray. She will be able to continue the great work they both achieved on the ray and on the Earth, while Saint Germain oversees the work of the seventh ray from his new position. Saint Germain describes Lady Portia as the lotus flower of the seventh ray of light.

Lady Portia is a mystical lady. She stands before us dressed in a violet sari with a matching head scarf draped over her head and around her neck. White crystals hang as decorative jewellery from her forehead.

She originates from a star within our universe and has studied on many planets such as Venus, and even the Earth in an eastern civilisation to gain her spiritual evolution. She embodies both the loving heart and the intuitive mind of the Creator, while devoting her energy to the distribution and understanding of the seventh ray of

115

light. Many on the Earth understand Lady Portia as being a member of the Board of Karma. This remains true: her work with the violet flame and ray of light only enhances her mission of assisting many in releasing karma caused by past lifetimes on the Earth.

The seventh ray, of a violet colour, is an extension of the third ray of light, benefiting greatly from the anchoring energy and manifestation the ray presents. The seventh ray is becoming a focal point for many as it holds the qualities within its light layers of the way in which we wish to exist on the Earth. This is named the new age. The light embodies the accelerated awareness, loving and spiritual actions which are goals many of us wish to achieve.

When we visit the seventh ray of light it is possible to ask Lady Portia to show us an example of the new age. It will be as if we are viewing a civilisation on a television screen, to help us understand the goals we are reaching for. In truth, the seventh ray embodies all the divine qualities that we have learnt from the one to six rays of light. The violet ray anchors all into its energy at different levels of frequency and vibration so we can access a new consciousness within our being and support our soul in continuing its expansion. When we view the example of the new age with Lady Portia we see a civilisation appearing as perfection on the Earth; the civilisation expresses peace, harmony and love toward one another. The spiritual awareness of every person is heightened as all channel and express the energy of the Creator in their own divine way.

We could compare this to the idealism that is associated with Atlantis. When souls on the Earth hunger to bring the civilisation of Atlantis back to the Earth, they may not realise that they are talking of the new age of the violet ray; a time where people are open and aware, obtaining the highest vibration a civilisation has ever achieved on the Earth. It is the violet ray that we must focus on anchoring into the world to create the spiritual reality within which we wish to exist; it is a form of heaven on the Earth.

We can imagine that if we have integrated the previous rays into our beings and realities then we will have achieved a state of being that is precious, enlightened and spiritually evolved, so the violet ray only accentuates and supports the advanced growth process of the soul.

It is appropriate that many see this ray as a magical energy; Lady Portia certainly embodies an air of mystery. It is the vast contrast between the way in which we live our lives now on the Earth and the idealism of a perfect spiritual civilisation living in a physical form that conjures up thoughts of magic. At present many of us are unable to comprehend the marvel of the Creator that can be anchored with the assistance of the violet ray of light. Mastery of one's being and vast spiritual awareness is a form of magic, compared with the lower vibrational awareness within which many live when their minds are focused only on physical matter.

The colour violet acts as a symbol of spiritual awareness, advancement and growth. By placing objects or wearing clothes of this colour, we can spark inspirational enlightened ideas and states of being. In invoking and anchoring the violet ray of light into our body, soul, aura and reality, we can create transformational effects upon our growth process, attracting what many would perceive as miracles. The violet ray enhances our own inner discipline, focus and concentration on the light of the Creator, our soul and its growth to develop rituals, practices and teachings of the purest divine nature to become a part of our lives and thought processes.

Magic in its purity is only a blissful energy that evolves from devoted spiritual practices and invocations of the light. Lady Portia especially draws on the indigo ray of Master Lanto to energise her ray with divine devotion; this intertwines with the goals of the seventh ray and allows many who invoke the violet ray to feel a unity or closeness with their soul and the Creator.

It is important for Lady Portia to anchor the violet energy onto and into the Earth as it can assist in eliminating negativity, false beliefs and the controlling influences of others, helping us to become free to follow a path of discovery with our soul and the Creator. Lady Portia's influence and work with the Earth is growing as more people awaken to the light, asking to be healed and cleansed of their past and the negativity that has evolved on the Earth. The violet energy of the new age and magical realities we dream of will begin to enter and anchor into individuals on the Earth who have gained an advanced spiritual state of being, allowing them to benefit from its support in raising their level of consciousness. There is still much work for us to achieve as a civilisation in order for us to see the new age existing within and before us as a new civilisation, or more appropriately an awakened civilisation existing in physical bodies.

As divine beings on the Earth we can invoke the seventh ray of light into our bodies by a simple request to Lady Portia to become integrated with the violet ray. The level of our awareness is not important as the violet ray will cleanse and heal our beings, inspiring and enlightening our minds to awaken beyond limitations, assisting us in anchoring greater love within our beings. The violet ray of light also activates and develops our psychic abilities and skills, encouraging them to manifest into our realities.

When we invoke the seventh ray of light we gain an understanding of who we really are and the vast power that exists within our physical bodies in accepting our soul or higher self. We will be able to comprehend this energy truly when we have integrated with the three main rays of light, as this will signify we have gained a high vibration with the ability to connect with the highest energy level of the violet ray of light.

Lady Portia holds great control over the violet flame of light, which has become an absolute and precious part of the seventh ray. It is Lady Portia, Archangel Zadkiel and Archangel Amethyst that we may call on to experience the energy of the violet flame. We can ask to visit the chamber of the violet flame in the spiritual ashram of the seventh ray during meditation or our sleep states.

A simple way to experience this cleansing energy is to invoke the violet flame while remaining consciously awake on the Earth. The violet flame will descend from its chamber, travelling down your body and then up again, returning to the seventh ray of light. This is a slow process, as it burns up the impurities within every aspect of the being and can eliminate disease from the body. It is important to respect the strength and power this flame possesses, experiencing its energy for five to ten minutes in a day. Abusing the flame's energy by invoking it constantly or unnecessarily throughout the day can and will only cause greater harm.

A cleansing process can be practised each day with the help of the violet flame of light. Its energy can be invoked to embody the entire Earth for a few moments during meditation to burn up all impurities on and within the Earth, helping to eliminate pollution of all kinds, especially the pollution of negative thoughts from humans that are scattered within the atmosphere. Removing the violet flame from the Earth after a few minutes and asking Lady Portia to pour the perfect amount of energy and light from the seventh ray into the Earth will assist in healing and uplifting the energy vibrations of humankind and

Mother Earth, opening up the chance for all to experience a heavenly reality on the Earth. After a cleansing process with the violet flame of light it is always essential to call upon the angelic love of Archangel Zadkiel and Archangel Amethyst, as the flame can strip our energy of nurturance, which can be replaced with the power of love.

We can feel secure with Lady Portia as the Chohan of the seventh ray because she is so deeply connected to the previous Master of this ray, Saint German. Her new position isn't by luck and is only slightly influenced by her previous work with this ray and the ray's Master.

Like all female Ascended Masters, Lady Portia is a manifestation of the Creator's feminine qualities; she is currently the only female Master of all the seven rays of light. Her presence among many male Masters is a symbol of the coming of feminine qualities to the Earth in an attempt to assist humans to love and care for each other, creating peace on the Earth, as well as to support Mother Earth. The Masters of the one to six rays of light each have a feminine aspect or anchor the feminine qualities of the Creator into their soul; they appear as male to us so we can appreciate their strength, power and determination.

Awakening on the Earth as a spiritual being is not easy when people around us are unable to see the truth of the Creator. It is therefore helpful for us as physical beings to feel the strength, support and immense power of these male aspect Masters surging through our bodies to enhance our faith and trust in the new path evolving before us. The seventh ray of light is the beginning of a line of female energies. With the greater presence of the feminine qualities of the Creator anchoring onto the Earth we will eventually become aware of a masculine and feminine Master governing each ray of light as one united energy.

We must understand that the seventh ray of light is assisting us in bringing in new high vibrations of energy onto the Earth. Mother Earth is evolving and it is Lady Portia who is supporting her in doing so. Lady Portia and Mother Earth are working closely to bring forth the feminine energies to assist people in abandoning the negative side of the masculine energy to replace it with love, peace, harmony, kindness, caring, growth and tranquillity. Lady Portia, united with the feminine and masculine Chohans, will lead the Earth in embodying love of the purest kind, anchoring it into the actions, thoughts and reactions between people to allow souls to blossom. This will then bring forth a balancing of these divine energies to allow harmony to be gained on the Earth, and each soul to embody both the positive masculine and feminine energies of the Creator. It is important we understand that all beings in the spiritual hierarchy come from a place of love within their souls and embody both the feminine and masculine positive energies of the Creator. The seventh ray is assisting greatly in this process of growth and integration on the Earth.

Allow Lady Portia to assist you in anchoring the seventh ray of light and its inspirational qualities into your being; permit her to help you in experiencing the violet flame of transmutation and revealing the Goddess within your being. She will also advance your spiritual and psychic abilities, if you ask her to. As you work with her divine and loving energies, you will assist Mother Earth in achieving the same advanced state of being that you aim to embody.

Archangel Zadkiel and his feminine aspect Archangel Amethyst are prominent figures on this ray of light and can be invoked to aid integration or work with the violet flame of light.

Let us welcome and honour Lady Portia in her new position and unite with her energy to receive the new age of the divine soul within our beings on the Earth.

CHAPTER 22

LADY NADA AND
THE EIGHTH RAY OF LIGHT

When we invoke Lady Nada, we may receive an image of a beautiful light-body lady kneeling down beside a pool of liquid or light of a sea-foam green colour. She reaches her cupped hands into the divine liquid and pours it over her head. This sea foam green or soft mint-coloured liquid, melts into every aspect of her being, glimmering and shining on and within her light body as she stands before us with her soul light blazing brightly into her limitless surroundings. Lady Nada wishes to demonstrate to us with this simple image the purpose and qualities of the eighth ray of light. Lady Nada's being is balanced, healed and cleansed of all impurities; she bathes in the light of the eighth ray constantly in order to embody its divine and sacred qualities.

When we connect with the eighth ray of light we receive an energy that expresses purity, high vibrations, cleanliness and oneness with the Creator and our soul. It is the purity within the soul of the mighty Creator that powerfully cleanses our energies and allows all contamination and pollution of numerous forms to fall away.

When we view all first seven rays of light we see that there are many cleansing rays assisting us in healing our beings. The second ray of light charges us with energy to break through the armour that blocks us from connecting with the Creator's light. The fourth ray of light assists us in removing any negative situations or obstacles to create harmony within and around us. The seventh ray of light holds the energy of the violet flame, removing all impurities from our bodies.

It seems unnecessary to have a ray completely devoted to cleansing when we can anchor healing into our beings from the rays two, four and seven, but the eighth ray has a particular mission that is supported by the previous cleansing rays of light. The rays two, four and seven show gradual cleansing processes of awakening, creating balance and removing fears. The eighth ray of light offers cleansing to the soul and spiritual bodies but doesn't have such an instant effect on the physical body as the other rays can. The eighth ray of light honours the soul and removes any blockages, fears or toxins from its path to allow it to swell and blossom into an expanded and limitless being. The energy is like a nourishing mother to souls, assisting them in developing to achieve their potential and the divine plan set before them.

When we invoke this sea-foam green energy, we are calling on Lady Nada to purify and nourish our souls and spiritual bodies, supporting the soul in its quest for integration. The eighth ray of light could be seen as a cleansing bath. From the moment we set foot in the ashram all impurities and unwanted energy fall away, allowing the soul to shine brightly, free from restrictions, blockages or barriers created by the physical and spiritual bodies. It is a cleansing process that supports the soul in its mission and goals of growth.

We can invoke Lady Nada and the sea-foam green light to pour into and over our body during meditation. The light will run through the body and aura carrying any negative energy into the Earth, where it will be transformed into light once more. This is a wonderful cleansing process and is almost like receiving a cleansing shower tumbling down and through our bodies. Our souls will naturally react to this energy, like a flower lifting its head to the sun.

Although the eighth ray doesn't work to heal the physical body, by cleansing the soul and spiritual bodies within the aura, we will naturally affect the physical body. Many illnesses and blockages develop from the outer bodies. As a last resort they manifest into the physical body as a warning that healing is needed. When we focus on using Lady Nada's energy to heal and nurture our soul we will automatically create a radiant physical body to live within.

It is most beneficial to visit Lady Nada's ashram on the inner planes once a week during your sleep state to maintain high vibrations, clean spiritual bodies and nurture the soul. Lady Nada's light will assist us in integrating the love and light of our souls into our physical bodies. She sees cleansing as a spiritual advancement: it is a tool to aid and enhance the development of the soul in a transformational way. Cleansing and healing will always be an aspect of our spiritual evolution, as we are constantly developing and changing with the necessity to shed old energy patterns. Lady Nada's ashram is a place of sanctuary for the inner soul; it is a tranquil and peaceful place where we can bathe in high vibrations to re-energise the soul, its light, love and influences on the physical personality.

As spiritual beings it is our aim to anchor all of the first seven rays of light into our being, understanding them and embodying their qualities in our every action on the Earth. Once this has been achieved we will have gained a significant growth process and can step onto the next stage of our growth, which combines the eight to twelve rays of light. These higher rays are available to everyone, but they work the closest with those who have realised a greater awareness and are preparing to integrate and embody their soul light fully.

The process of integrating with the soul is one that is developed in different ways by all the rays of light. We must remember that all rays are equal, they just work with different aspects of our beings. We will only truly connect with the eighth ray of light when we have integrated and mastered the first seven rays. The influence of the eighth ray of light could be described as a nirvana, a transcendental or freedom experience, as we are able to let everything flow away from us and exist in a contented state of peace and purity.

It is Lady Nada's mission to develop the growth previously attained by the soul, and to focus the skills, wisdom and love that exist within or have been gained during evolution to increase the loving power of the soul. Through her cleansing process Lady Nada peels away the exterior shields surrounding the soul to allow its full power and light to emerge and begin to blossom.

Lady Nada is not alone in her work on the eighth ray of light; she has many light bodies and Masters assisting her with her work. As with the other rays of light, there are many levels to the eighth ray which can be accessed. Cleansing and healing can take many forms and may be expressed in many ways. Lady Nada draws on the energy of the sixth ray of light to enhance the power of her ray; the devotional energy of Master Lanto surrounds souls in a comforting energy and inspires them to emerge from their shields of protection to advance further.

Lady Nada is from the planet Venus. She is an aspect of the soul of Master Sananda or Master Jesus as we know him on the Earth. Indeed, she has been named his twin flame or the feminine aspect of his soul, and could be known as a 'Kumara', which is the name of the souls that came from Venus to assist the Earth. Lady Nada served on the sixth ray of light when Master Sananda was Chohan, embodying the energy of devotion which she brings to the eighth ray of light as well as the energy of the Christ.

Her presence on the eighth ray is essential as she brings forth the energy of the Goddess to the Earth with Lady Portia, Lady Mary, Lady Vessa, Lady Quan Yin and Lady Pallas Athena who are the Chohans of the higher rays. It is appropriate that Lady Nada is a member of the Boards of Karma. Her work on the Board and as Chohan of the eighth ray of light allows her to eliminate fear, pain and suffering from every aspect of the being to reveal the divine within.

Working alongside Lady Nada and charging energy into the eighth ray of light are the Pleiadians. They are known to us as Extraterrestrial Beings, but they are advanced civilisations that are extending their light body hands to us to aid us in evolving spiritually. They see us as being asleep and wish to awaken us to the truth that exists around us. The Pleiadians exist on an open star cluster in the constellation of Taurus; they are among the nearest star cluster to the Earth known as the seven sisters or the M45. The Pleiadians have made many connections with channels and light workers on the Earth; they combine the love of the Creator and advanced technology to develop the spiritual existence of their civilisation. The Pleiadians have space ships allowing them to travel to the Earth whenever they feel their help is needed. They channel their energy into Lady Nada's ashram to enhance their connection with the Earth and to create a special haven where we can connect and communicate with them in a place of safety.

They understand the fear that some humans hold towards Extraterrestrials and so use the eighth ray of light as a base for a divine connection to be made. Their connection with the eighth ray of light and Lady Nada is not by chance. They have a mission that complements the work of the eighth ray of light and allows them to work with students visiting the ray. The Pleiadians wish to prepare each incarnate soul on the Earth, who has awoken to the light of the Creator, to integrate and embody their soul or soul group. They offer many techniques and practices, working personally with the incarnate souls, supporting the person's preparations with the high frequency energy of the Pleiadians.

Lady Nada, the Masters working on her ray, and the Pleiadians work together to cleanse and prepare a soul to emerge and integrate with its physical body or light body, depending on its existence. We can invoke both Lady Nada and the Pleiadians to assist us in our spiritual cleansing processes, asking them to assist us in preparing our soul to integrate with our light bodies and physical bodies. They will channel the energy of the eighth ray into our beings to assist this growth process.

The eighth ray of a sea-foam green colour is an excellent place to visit, and a high vibrational energy to anchor into our beings to accelerate the spiritual evolution of our souls. We will experience only love and purity from this ray of light, originating from the depths of the Creator's mighty soul. For those who wish to connect on a deeper level with the Pleiadians, understanding their civilisation and integrating their energy into their being, the eighth ray of light is the perfect place to visit and connect with. By linking with the energy of the eighth ray we will automatically receive some of the Pleiadians' energy, but when we ask for the Pleiadians to enter into our lives and assist our spiritual evolution, a deeper bond is formed.

The Pleiadians come from a place of love and wish to assist us in healing our beings. There is no need to fear their presence or their evolved nature, they only want to help us in any way they can. If you feel a bond with these beings but can feel fearful emotions building within you, then you can ask Lady Nada to assist in forming a bond. She will ensure your safety at all times.

The angelic representatives of the eighth ray of light are Archangel Jeremiel and Archangel Josephine. It is their mission to help us to integrate the cleansing and purifying qualities of the eighth ray into our physical lives and realities to dissolve fears, anxieties and worries, while encouraging a cleansing or de-cluttering of our reality. The Archangels wish to assist us in purifying and simplifying our physical path and journey on the Earth.

Let us allow the cleansing and healing light of the eighth ray to pour over and into our beings as we invite Lady Nada and the Pleiadians to assist our soul in its spiritual evolution on the Earth and in the spiritual planes.

CHAPTER 23

LADY MARY AND
THE NINTH RAY OF LIGHT

The preparations of the eighth ray for the soul or monad aspect merge are enhanced and developed further in the ninth ray of light, assisting the light body to anchor into the physical body or energy body. The ninth ray offers us a unique experience of discovering our soul and its abilities with greater depth; exploration and understanding of the soul is seen as a predominant stage of integrating with the soul and the Creator. The light of the ninth ray is of a blue-green colour that simultaneously presents the colours individually and merged. The ashram can be described as a meadow with luscious green grass and crystal blue sky.

The light of the eighth, ninth and tenth rays relates to and facilitates the growth of the soul. Together the rays assist aspects of the soul in merging with its current embodiment. For the more advanced students the focus is on integrating with aspects of the monad or soul group. It is because of this mission that these rays are known as the higher rays. Once we have passed through the ashram of Lady Nada and her cleansing bath, then we are open and receptive to work with Lady Mary and the ninth ray of light that furthers the soul's growth by anchoring the energy of the light body into the body and soul, while encouraging exploration of the soul's consciousness.

The soul by now is radiating its energy into its surroundings through the focus of the mind, attracting the bright vibrant planetary light body, which is a grid-work of light within which the soul exists when living in the spiritual world. Anchoring the planetary light body is very important as it is a preparation for ascension. We must connect and anchor this light body into our beings to become accustomed to its energy, ensuring we have a safe temple within which to remain when we leave our physical bodies to ascend or evolve into a new state of realisation. Allowing the planetary light body to anchor into the physical body secures greater light into the body and soul, assisting and guiding the soul and physical personality to receive and accept a new level of consciousness: it can act as an introduction to a new awareness and energy vibration.

At this stage we may even begin to switch between two levels of consciousness because of the presence of the light body. This higher consciousness will only be gained when a full soul merge is achieved, but it can be accessed during meditation. Integration of the light body is almost a test to evaluate whether the soul itself is ready to move to a state of greater or full integration; the Masters of the ninth ray are able to determine whether extra growth or light is needed to support the expansion of the soul.

Full integration is achievable, but we must remember that this is only at a planetary level. Many more states of soul and monad merges and light body integrations must be achieved in order to become fully united with the Creator. We see the integration of our souls with our physical personalities as a pinnacle point in our processes of growth leading to full soul merge, but in truth it is only the beginning of numerous aspects of integration.

The greatest gift that the ninth ray offers to us is the ability to discover our soul, accepting its wealth of wisdom, abilities, skills and profound guidance, as well as to gain a new understanding of our past lifetimes on the Earth and future purposes. By existing in our soul light while anchoring the ninth ray we are able to acknowledge the wealth of enlightenment that we hold.

It is Lady Mary who is named as Chohan of the ninth ray of light of a blue-green colour. She has many spiritual names, such as Mother Mary, Sister Mary, Archangel Mary and Mary Queen of the Angels, but for her position as Chohan of this ray of light she wishes to be named Lady Mary, to show her deep connection with the other Chohans and Masters of the rays.

Lady Mary has incarnated onto the Earth as the mother of Jesus, and Isis the mother of Horus; her past lifetimes show that she is a caring, compassionate and nurturing soul who wishes to act as a kind mother to all souls in their growth process of expansion. Lady Mary is a beautiful feminine light being. Her facial features are perfection as bliss, joy and a loving sense of humour emanate from her soul. She can sometimes manifest before us, when invoked, in a deep blue cloak and hood which appear to embody the light rays of the universe. The smile that she bestows on us when pushing her hood back reaches out and touches the very core of our soul with pure love. Lady Mary appears to many people on the Earth, offering and sharing her love. It is as though her spirit walks alongside humankind, assisting those in need of divine guidance and inspiration.

Lady Mary holds a deep connection with the Angelic Kingdom, which was evident in her past lifetimes on the Earth. The Creator in the past has permitted her to follow the path of an Archangel due to her intense devotion to assisting others and acting as a messenger of the Creator. Lady Mary is the twin flame or feminine aspect working with Archangel Raphael to heal humankind, diminishing negativity and fear to allow the soul to flourish. Her Archangel presence is another aspect of her soul. While her command as ninth ray Chohan is by the manifestation of her Ascended Master self, it is just one aspect of the numerous personalities of her soul. Her presence on the ninth ray of light assists her greatly in her work with Archangel Raphael and the healing Angels. Healing brings joy, and a quality of the ninth ray is pure joy.

Archangel Raphael and Archangel Mary work intensively with the fifth ray of light of an orange colour governed by Master Hilarion; this is the ray of science, or investigation of the soul, and it is deeply connected to the work of the ninth ray. Many of the practices and information discovered regarding the soul on the fifth ray of light are applied to the ninth ray teachings to assist in preparing for the soul or monad merge on the tenth ray of light. We can see that Lady Mary's connection with the fifth and ninth ray is not by accident. She has a wonderful gift for nurturing souls, and this skill weaves into the ninth and fifth rays of light.

Master Hilarion benefits from the higher cleansing and blissful rays that emanate from the ninth ray of light, using this energy to fuel, guide and encourage his scientific Masters in remaining connected with their own souls and the soul of the mighty Creator.

Again we see how all the rays of light assist each other and cannot function without the support and unity of the other rays. We can also understand how it is possible for a Master to work on and with many different rays of light. By placing them in departments we are actually misinterpreting the limitless energy of each of their souls and the rays of light, but at the same time it is important for us to understand whom we can connect with to assist us in our spiritual evolution.

Lady Mary anchors the energy of the entire Angelic Kingdom into the ninth ray of light. The Angels are connected to all rays of light, but

Lady Mary allows her students to feel the full love and support of the Angelic Kingdom as it is an effective way of nourishing the soul in its process of growth. The qualities of the Angelic Kingdom as messengers and carriers of the Creator's love are anchored into the student's light body and physical body on this blue-green ray of light to raise the energy vibration and increase the student's light quotient beyond their current existence. We cannot fault the energy of the Angels as their work is selfless and they are devoted to the light.

It is on the ninth ray that we can truly understand and connect with the souls and energies of the Angels and Archangels. Lady Mary's twin flame, Archangel Raphael, also works on the ninth ray of light; in fact, many Archangels anchor their energy into the ninth ray of light because of the great presence of the angelic energy within the ashram.

When we visit the ninth ray ashram in our sleep states we can bathe in the blue-green energy to nourish and enhance the loving power of our souls. Some people find it beneficial during one sleep state or meditation first to visit the eighth ray of light before continuing to the ninth ray of light, to ensure they are cleansed and focused, ready to work on the development and expansion of their soul when they arrive in the ninth ray. This is one of the reasons for the deep bond between the eighth and ninth rays of light.

If you wish to practise this, then before you fall asleep at night or before meditation, ask to be taken first to the eighth ray of light to receive complete cleansing with Lady Nada, and then the ninth ray of light to discover your soul with Lady Mary.

We can anchor the blue-green energy of the ninth ray of light into our bodies and every aspect of our beings by a simple invocation to Lady Mary. She will pour the light of her ashram continuously into our bodies and auras to enhance our vibrations. The blue-green energy will especially accumulate in our souls, promoting progression and expansion.

The effects and influences of Lady Mary's energy do not just assist the soul, but promote greater joy and pure bliss to emanate from within our beings. When we feel down, upset or need a boost, we can call on Lady Mary and her ninth ray energy to fill us with the joy of the Creator, so we can see and experience joy in every situation in our lives and every action we make. The joy we receive stems from the Creator's and Lady Mary's soul, it enhances the pure joyous energy already within our beings, assisting and guiding us to become continuously connected with the joy of our souls.

Joy is a form of love. We all need to experience joy and fun in our lives, otherwise our energy vibrations and faith can plummet, causing us to disconnect from our souls and the soul of the Creator. We can ask Lady Mary to send a light beam of joy into our hearts and souls to boost the body of love within us. She will wrap us in a blanket of joy and love when we are ill or feel tender, because joy is healing to all aspects of the being. When we invoke Lady Mary, she can fill whole rooms full of people and buildings with the purest energy of joy, instigating a mass rise in energy vibration.

Lady Mary can assist us in changing the attitudes of others towards us with her special energy of joy. The presence of joy on the Earth and within our souls can remove the qualities of judgment, harm, violence and negativity to allow love to triumph. When invoking Lady Mary and her blue-green energy specifying that we wish to embody joy of the highest vibration, we may find that we are bubbling with happiness and delight for no physical reason; this energy can assist in healing illnesses and fuelling the mind's tool of manifestation.

Within Lady Mary's ashram are present many Masters and Angels working to assist visiting students, but the energy of the Sirian beings also boosts the ninth ray energy and light. As the Pleiadians assist Lady Nada and anchor their energy into the eighth ray of light, the beings of Sirius anchor their light into Lady Mary's ashram. Their purpose is very similar to the Pleiadians; they wish to assist humans in their spiritual evolution and find that by anchoring their energy into the ninth ray ashram they can create a neutral ground for us to connect with the Sirian energy, beginning to work with their civilisation. During the exposition of Master Kuthumi's existence, we discussed the star of Sirius, which resembles a spiritual university where beings throughout the universe gather to advance their spiritual awareness and learning.

Sirius is one of the paths that lead us closer to unity with the Creator and discovering our inner truth. The Sirians are an evolved civilisation of beings living on a star in the constellation Canis Major, which is approximately 8.6 light years from the Earth. They are devoting much of their time to assisting us on the Earth with our evolution and are an influential part of the training of souls once they have ascended from their physical bodies and the Earth.

There is a special reason for the connection of the Sirian energy with the ninth ray of light; the Sirians offer many souls the tools, information and techniques to accelerate their growth process. Anchoring these into the ninth ray energy aids the soul's process of discovery, which is the main purpose of the ninth ray, helping us to find out more about ourselves, energies, past lifetimes, skills, connections, and the wealth of knowledge held within our soul. The ninth ray enables us to learn, realise and uncover the most sacred part of our existence, the aspect of the Creator that we hold within us.

When we visit the ninth ray of light we can meet with some Sirian beings that have been assigned to work with Lady Mary, and can ask them to assist us in expanding our awareness to support the growth of our souls. There are many lectures and workshops given by the Sirian beings that can be attended on the ninth ray of light, overseen by Lady Mary, which focus on anchoring the light body, exploring the soul and preparing the soul or monad for integration.

If these classes and lectures aren't sufficient for our growth, or greater time and wisdom is needed before progression, then with Lady Mary's permission we may be transported during our sleep states from the ninth ray of light to the star of Sirius to attend the appropriate lectures or to speak with certain Masters. Master Kuthumi has been known to welcome the students of the ninth ray of light who visit Sirius for advanced wisdom and enlightenment. Master Kuthumi assists because of his connection with the Earth and the second ray of light. His loving qualities help students to feel comfortable and safe. He also guides them to the appropriate Sirian Masters or lectures; many other Masters and Sirian beings assist in this process. The ninth ray of light could be named the ray of learning, but this process of growth is not to illumine the mind but to expand the energy of the soul within the physical or light body.

If you feel you wish to create a connection with the Sirians and want to ask them to assist your growth, then the ninth ray is a wonderful place for this bond to form, as Lady Mary acts, as always, as a mother to all souls, overseeing everything that occurs in her ashram. The Sirians anchor the light of the Galactic Core and Universal Logos Melchizedek into their energy; this high vibrational cosmic energy is charged into Lady Mary's ashram, making it a place of sacred energy and cosmic connections.

Allow Lady Mary and the ninth ray of light to assist in developing the divine within your being, anchoring your planetary light body to enhance further growth, while allowing you to discover and learn about the sacred energies of the Creator within you. Allow her motherly loving energy to nourish and heal your soul while helping you understand the truth of your being and the mission of your soul. Her joy will light up any room and ignite the flame of love and happiness within your being.

We must remember that we can call on her as a loving mother, as a sister, an Archangel and a guiding light. She is always available to assist us in any way, as she introduces and anchors the energy of the Angelic Kingdom and the Sirian beings into our lives and souls through the ninth ray of light. Let us honour the unconditional love and the Goddess energy she shares with each and every soul on the Earth, and invoke her presence as a spiritual mentor to aid the spiritual evolution of our souls.

CHAPTER 24
LADY AND MASTER ANDROMEDA AND THE TENTH RAY OF LIGHT

The tenth ray of light is a continuation of the ninth ray of light; the energies of this ray are still focused on the soul or monad and their integration at a planetary level. The tenth ray of light instigates the soul or monad merge after preparation on the eighth and ninth rays. The feeling of the tenth ray energy is very different from the other rays, and this is one of the reasons why Lady Mary has been placed as Chohan of the ninth ray of light, to comfort and support an individual's progression to the tenth ray.

The tenth ray of light is of a pearlescent colour symbolising the unity of all the previous rays within the tenth ray ashram. This ray acts as a cocoon when the student first steps into the ashram; it creates a high vibration to support the soul or monad as it begins to pour its energy into the light body and the physical body on the Earth. Great support and love emanate from this cocoon of pearlescent light as any negative thoughts or doubts could hinder the merging of the soul or monad aspect and send the student back to the ninth ray of light to continue its growth with Lady Mary for a further period. Of course, Lady Mary doesn't allow her students to enter or invoke the tenth ray without being perfectly sure they are ready to experience the next stages of growth, not just on the tenth ray of light but on the eleventh and twelfth rays, as these two higher rays continue the process of soul or monad integration once it has began on the tenth ray.

Through a student's work with the eighth and ninth rays they would have become accustomed to working with light beings known to us as Extraterrestrials, discovering that these civilisations within our universe assist in the growth of humanity on the Earth. It will be of no surprise that the preparations in connecting with the Pleiadians and the Sirian energies have the purpose of expanding our awareness and removing fears, aiding us in accepting the tenth ray of light solely governed by Extraterrestrial Beings from Andromeda.

The Andromedans are one of the most evolved civilisations working with humankind on the Earth; their civilisation is very large, inhabiting the Andromeda galaxy in the constellation of Andromeda. It is a spiral galaxy approximately 2.5 million light years away from the Earth. The technology of the Andromedans is far beyond anything we have experienced on the Earth, but this advancement in their civilisation, unlike on the Earth, is supported and fuelled by the positive light of the Creator. They are continually connected to the Creator's mighty soul and understand that this is the only way for them to exist in harmony. The Andromedans also hold a balance between the feminine and masculine qualities of the Creator and all exist as equal light souls.

These wise beings have much to teach humanity, but it is very difficult for us to remain opened-minded to them when nearly all of us have been programmed to be fearful of Extraterrestrials, which creates a barrier between us and these divine civilisations who are trying to assist us. The understanding of Extraterrestrial Beings working on our higher rays of light may cause some people to doubt their faith in the Creator and their spiritual evolution. This fear has stopped people on the Earth from progressing spiritually; they are unable to accept the higher rays because of the presence of the Extraterrestrials working on these rays. This is precisely the mission of controlling authorities on the Earth; the fear that we hold towards Extraterrestrials retains us under control and ensures we don't merge with our souls or monads to gain freedom at a planetary level or within our physical bodies, as we would become too powerful.

It is important for us to understand there are negative Extraterrestrials, but there is a larger number of positive and loving Extraterrestrials working to aid the growth of the Earth. Many Masters on the rays one to seven are Extraterrestrials, originating from planets and stars within our universe, but they hide behind the masks of their last incarnations on the Earth to assist humans in accepting them. They aren't trying to deceive us but are lovingly protecting us until we open to greater illumination and comprehension. Every single being on the Earth and in the universe is a manifestation of the Creator. By discovering more about the Extraterrestrials we are able to apply this understanding to every light being we meet, accepting them and their existence wholeheartedly.

Many people on the Earth have tried to place different Ascended Masters on the tenth ray of light to disguise the presence of the

Andromedans, but it is Lady and Master Andromeda who are the Chohans of this ray of pearlescent light. Lady and Master Andromeda are not Ascended Masters from the Earth but are a female and male energy that have been chosen from the Andromeda civilisation to work as leaders of their team in the tenth ray ashram. They have been given the titles Lady and Master to show their unity with the other rays of light and their Chohans. Their team working on the tenth ray of light has also been selected from Andromeda because of their gifts of communicating with souls on the Earth, their loving qualities, and their ability to facilitate a soul or monad merge. The tenth ray allows the Andromedans to connect with the Earth. Their main existence and home is in the Andromeda galaxy, but they have many starships that travel around the universe collecting valuable information to accelerate the growth of our planet, as well as their civilisation.

The Divine Director of Rays within the Planetary Logos Ashram acts as an overseer to all the higher rays, conveying instructions and the divine plan of the Creator for the Earth to Lady and Master Andromeda. Lord Buddha and many other Masters in the spiritual hierarchy constantly observe the tenth ray of light; this is not because they do not trust the Andromedans, but because they are fascinated by the work they achieve in their ashram of pearlescent light. This ray is a place of major transformation; most Ascended Masters working in the higher levels of the spiritual hierarchy have passed through this ray to experience the merging of the soul or monad with the physical or light body.

The soul or planetary monad merge is also a process of uniting with the ten rays of light of the Creator's divine soul, and later the eleventh and twelfth rays to complete the planetary integration. The very essence of the tenth ray of light is acceptance; this is a quality that we explore fully within the pearlescent light. Acceptance allows us to fuse, join and bring together our energies to make a more complete source of Creator's light within us. The tenth ray of light also assists us in accepting the discoveries we have made within the teachings of the ninth ray ashram.

It is Lady Andromeda who presents her name to us, as she holds the energy of the Goddess within her and is working to balance the feminine and masculine energies on the Earth with the other female Chohans of the higher rays of light. Her Name is Lady Vessa.

The male energy working with her is reluctant to give his name, as the focus of these rays is currently on the feminine energy. This will of course change as the Goddess energy of the Creator becomes anchored into the Earth and its inhabitants, and the male and female energies become balanced. Although Lady Vessa has a greater influence on the Earth, within the tenth ray ashram Master and Lady Andromeda are equal; they combine their energies as an example of the balance between the feminine and masculine qualities that is present within the energy of the Creator.

Lady and Master Andromeda work from their souls, hearts and minds. They cocoon the student or soul in love of the purest kind and direct the soul or monad to truly begin its integration, its acceptance of the masculine and feminine energies, of the rays and the physical or light bodies, depending on the level of the student. They assist in creating a connection between the mind and the manifestation of the soul so they act and exist as one. Light beams from both the mind and the soul in perfect harmony; this is a process of receiving a new level of consciousness. Lady and Master Andromeda and their team work with the student soul to ensure this integration remains stable.

The student then moves on to attend lectures, workshops and personal meetings with the Andromedan team to ensure the safety of the new aspect of their soul or monad integration. If the student is to return to his or her Earth body then much of this preparation is needed, and it continues each time the physical body sleeps at night. This is not a quick process. There isn't a flash of light and a new soul or monad merge has occurred. The process can take years and sometimes lifetimes; but of course, the speed of spiritual growth is quickening on the Earth, causing more students to gain a high enough vibration to gather on the tenth ray of light. At the highest level of this ray the soul is prepared to experience the next ray of light. Some students also have the opportunity to visit the home of the Andromedans, studying with members of the civilisation who hold different roles and wisdom to the beings working on the tenth ray of light.

The tenth ray of light is open to those who have studied with Lady Nada and Lady Mary on the previous rays of light and are ready to experience the anchoring of an aspect of their soul or monad within their current existence. To visit this ray of light we need a certain amount of awakening to comprehend the process occurring, but we must remember that on some level we have already achieved this, as spiritual growth is simply a process of realisation. The tenth ray can be invoked by all, as when you allow its pearlescent light to flow into your body, it will help to bind all energies, consciousness and vibrations you have recently worked with, allowing acceptance and completion of numerous stages of your spiritual advancement. If you are having difficulty accepting energies, understandings or aspects of your being, you can invoke the tenth ray to be of assistance.

There is a chamber within the tenth ray of light which is devoted to assisting humankind to connect with and understand the Andromedan civilisations. If we feel a deep connection with them, it is this chamber we are permitted to visit in our sleep states or in meditation. It is important to ask our personal Angels to guide us and ensure we are safe and protected.

We must always state that we only wish to visit the tenth ray and the Andromedans if our souls believe it will be beneficial for our spiritual development. Visiting the Andromedan chamber of learning and understanding is an exciting opportunity as they have much wisdom and a vast comprehension of our universe that they wish to share with us. Within this special Andromedan chamber, the Andromedan team will guide and assist us to access and progress to this stage of soul or monad merging. They will suggest a variety of rays of light and Masters who can assist us in progressing eventually to study on the tenth ray of light. Their spiritual advice is engaging, as they can specify the correct path through the rays of light that will aid an individual's soul or monad merge.

They wish to help us in any way they can, whether it is to advise us on our spiritual paths and education or to aid us in understanding their civilisation with greater clarity. We can invoke the tenth ray of light to anchor and channel into our beings throughout the day. This will raise our energy vibrations, increase our connections with all the rays of light, support the growth of our souls, and most importantly remove the barriers of fear towards Extraterrestrials. We must remember this energy is of a high vibration and our guides will direct us to use this ray of light to aid our spiritual evolution when the time is right.

Lady Vessa Andromeda and Master Andromeda are divine and loving beings; the wisdom they hold and wish to share with us is vast and is greatly needed on the Earth. They are a symbol of the balance, harmony, wisdom and the bright blazing light we are all striving to gain. Let us welcome them into our lives, accept their loving presence within our spiritual hierarchy, understanding the greatness they achieve. The tenth ray is a pinnacle point of the soul or monad acceptance, the rays and the spiritual hierarchy, as it integrates all energies into its teachings and practices.

CHAPTER 25

LADY QUAN YIN AND
THE ELEVENTH RAY OF LIGHT

Lady Quan Yin is a Goddess, Ascended Master, an embodiment of enlightenment, and a compassionate mother to the inhabitants of the entire Earth. She loves, nurtures and encourages every soul who is open to her light on the Earth. Her energy and focus are very similar to Lady Mary's; both embody love of the purest kind and anchor the energy of the Goddess onto the Earth.

The gracious Lady Quan Yin acts as a spiritual mentor to many light workers on the Earth. She would share her wisdom and love with the entire world if she could, her soul is that devoted to the Earth and the ascension process of each individual. Lady Quan Yin is an enlightened beacon of light, following the path of aiding her fellow beings on the Earth to evolve, rather than continuing with her own accelerated growth. Her love for humankind is immense. She is discovering greater enlightenment and growth by dedicating her energy to helping her brothers and sisters on the Earth and in the spiritual hierarchy at a planetary level.

Lady Quan Yin is deeply connected and integrated with the Planetary Logos Lord Buddha; she is a feminine aspect of his energy. While Lord Buddha oversees the spiritual energies of the Earth, Lady Quan Yin anchors her own feminine energies and Lord Buddha's masculine energies into the eleventh ray of light and the Board of Karma. Quan Yin allocates much of her time to assisting souls on the Earth in resolving their karmic issues, inspiring them to break free from the boundaries of karma.

Lady Quan Yin presents herself as the Chohan of the eleventh ray of light, which is of an orange and pink colour. The higher vibrations of this ray are represented by a peach colour. The eleventh ray of light holds deep connections with the eight to ten rays of light as all are focused on the soul or monad merge and integration. Lady Quan Yin continues to support this process of the soul merge, while also assisting students to accept and become accustomed to their new consciousness and high vibration. The qualities of the eleventh ray of light are embodiment, anchoring, incarnation, and existing as the higher vibrations discovered in the previous rays.

The eleventh ray of light is akin to a magical and beautiful garden within an unlimited light capsule of a pink and orange colour. As we walk through the garden it emanates the purity of the Creator's love, demonstrating to the soul that every aspect of life is a manifestation of love. This lesson has been explored in previous rays of light but has a greater significance on the eleventh ray, after the soul or monad aspect merge, as the soul is able to fully experience, accept and anchor love deeper within the physical and light bodies.

Many of us on the Earth see Mother Nature's manifestation of plants, animals and trees as the beauty and magnificence of the Creator. This is one of the reasons the eleventh ray of light shows itself to us as a garden of love. It is a place where the student can rest and recuperate after the soul or monad merge, and the intensity of the tenth ray of light with Lady Vessa Andromeda and Master Andromeda. It is similar to a healing sanctuary or temple, where peace, love and tranquillity gradually seep gently into the physical or light body and soul; we could compare this to a place of heavenly qualities.

The eleventh ray of light appears as a place of rest after the immense work that has taken place, where healing, balancing, anchoring and acceptance of one's achievements and the influence of the soul can be explored and understood from a new perspective. It is at this stage that the physical body, if still in manifestation on the Earth, will receive greater light, high vibrations and healing from the eleventh ray of light to enhance the soul or monad merge. The eleventh ray at the lowest energy level is a place of rest where one can simply adore the beauty and loving energy of the ray, while embracing the new energy of beauty that has blossomed from within.

The student is embraced in Quan Yin's loving arms, as the pink ray of light symbolising the purity of the Creator's love seeps slowly and gently into the soul. This energy of love is of a higher energy vibration than the energies of love anchored into the previous rays, suggesting that the embodiment of the eleventh ray loving energy will be a process of sacred heavenly enlightenment, assisting the student in surging forward to gain new realities and aspects of unity with the Creator.

We can connect and invoke the divine energy of pink light from the

140

eleventh ray ashram to anchor into our beings and assist us in embodying the love of the Creator. The pink component of the eleventh ray is used and channelled through many Angels who direct it into the Earth. The colour pink is a symbol of love and healing, even peace and harmony. This is why it is anchored into the eleventh ray: in preparation for absorbing the Christ Consciousness; a high vibration of love from the Christ Ashram and the twelfth ray of light. Quan Yin uses the pink ray of her ashram to assist her work with the Boards of Karma, to eliminate negative or dark energy and prepare people to anchor the Christ Consciousness into their beings and souls.

The orange ray of light that merges with the pink light is drawn from the highest vibration of the fifth ray of light which is associated with soul discovery. Lady Quan Yin and Master Hilarion have a deep connection between their ashrams and the loving presence of their souls; they both work closely with the student or soul to achieve enlightenment and embodiment at the highest planetary level within their ashrams. The orange ray of light actually opens several doors to students working with the eleventh ray, allowing them to obtain new wisdom not just from the planetary spiritual hierarchy but also from the solar level and some of its Masters.

New wisdom is brought forth from many Masters and Extraterrestrial Beings through Lady Quan Yin and her team on the eleventh ray to enlighten the student further. With the new presence of the soul or monad and a higher conscious level, a recap of the soul's previous knowledge is given now that they are able to fully digest and comprehend the information, connecting it with their life on the Earth or in the spiritual world. This is the process of embodiment.

A true comprehension of the spiritual world is also gained and a map can be made to aid the soul's achievement of goals and desires for learning. The soul is explored at an even deeper level than it has been before, as the mind is now more receptive to the soul and responds directly to its influence, rather than the dampening authority of the ego. Of course, the ego is ever present. Even when a Master has evolved to cosmic heights the ego can still be evident on some level, but only as a small fraction of the negative thoughts that are experienced on the Earth.

The main influence of the orange and pink light is to assist individuals to anchor and embody new aspects of their soul at greater depth than has been experienced before. Although integration has occurred, there is still plenty to realise within the limitless energy of the soul. A process of aligning energies to the soul begins. The merged pink and orange rays of light form a powerful high vibrational ashram where greater enlightenment can be gained, and they can even instigate the next process of the soul merge at a solar level.

The eleventh ray of light can assist in embodying, anchoring and integrating with the energy of Mother Earth. We would imagine that to ascend we must free ourselves of the Earth's physical energy, but by embodying the love of Mother Earth's spiritual aspect we can receive greater love, allowing us to share this divine loving energy with the inhabitants of the Earth, our brothers and sisters. Embodying the energy of Mother Earth will raise the vibration of the Earth and reward us with a greater feeling of love, unity and acceptance of the Creator's energy within our beings.

Lady Quan Yin teaches us that we are all manifestations of love. We cannot forget that the Creator exists within Mother Earth and how Mother Earth cares for all of us as a loving Mother. When we accept the energy of Mother Earth and acknowledge the pure love of our fellow human beings, we are accepting the love of the Creator. It is Lady Quan Yin's devotion to the Earth that encourages her to teach this lesson to humankind, whatever the level of their spiritual growth.

The energies of Lady Quan Yin and the eleventh ray of light are open to everyone to invoke as they will nurture the soul within the physical body, act as a supportive energy for spiritual practices and anchor greater love into the being. Because of its peaceful and tranquil energies, the eleventh ray of light is also ideal to invoke during meditation or when clarity is needed to overcome negative situations. The sacred energy assists with the embodiment of energies, consciousness and wisdom with which we are aligning during our present reality, and it can strengthen our connections with our guides, the Masters and the Creator.

It is interesting to note that the quality of the tenth ray is acceptance, while the energy of the eleventh ray is of embodiment. These teachings seem identical, but when explored hold the key to true integration. Lady Quan Yin's position on the Board of Karma means she is open to invocations from anyone in need of healing and cleansing. She will be honoured to pour the pink energy of the eleventh ray into the person to heal and nurture in any way she can.

Visiting the eleventh ray ashram is acceptable during our sleep states or meditation. As Lady Quan Yin is open to discussing our spiritual evolution with us, she is eager for us to view and experience the garden of love that exists within her ashram to gain a piece of heaven, while our bodies rest on the Earth. She shares her compassionate energy and wise intuition with everyone. She will act as a spiritual mother and guide to any soul that resonates with her energy and will direct many students to connect with certain rays, as well as her own, in order to enhance their spiritual evolution.

Lady Quan Yin is probably the most accessible of all the Chohans on the higher rays of light. Her ashram is a healing sanctuary and a temple of peace that is focused on the souls who have achieved integration, but it can be accessed by any soul of any vibration, as she will ensure that the correct quantity of energy is obtained by each individual. Lady Quan Yin ensures she can be accessed by souls incarnate on the Earth as she wishes to anchor the love, compassion and peace of the Creator and the Planetary Logos Lord Buddha onto the Earth, combined with the Goddess energy that she anchors with her sister Chohans of the higher rays of light.

It is important to notice the position of Lady Quan Yin on the eleventh ray of light and Lady Mary on the ninth ray of light. Both are loving, motherly figures, placed either side of the Andromedan energy. Lady Mary has been placed on the ninth ray as a loving mother to nurture and prepare the student to enter and work with the tenth ray of light, while Lady Quan Yin inhabits the eleventh ray to ensure the student's soul remains stable and is encouraged further. The bond between these female Chohans stems deeper, as Lady Quan Yin is known as a divine mother for the eastern civilisation and religions, while Lady Mary is the divine mother for the western civilisations and religions. Their deep bond symbolises to us the unity that can be formed on the Earth, showing how love prevails over any restrictions or beliefs that may exist on the Earth. Just as Lord Buddha and Lord Maitreya demonstrate the great unity within the spiritual hierarchy, so Lady Mary and Lady Quan Yin express the unity between the feminine energies of the eastern and western civilisations. This is the reason why Lady Mary has been accepted onto the Board of Karma, so that Lady Quan Yin and she can release the karma being created due to the suffering not only of both western and eastern civilisations, but indeed the entire planet. Their love, grace and compassion united as one seep into the Earth to heal and awaken humankind to their actions.

Lady Quan Yin also forms a bond with Lady Portia, Chohan of the seventh ray of light. Both Chohans are focused on bringing the new age, the new level of consciousness to the Earth. Lady Quan Yin channels the energy of the eleventh ray and the united higher rays, eight to twelve, into Lady Portia's ashram not only to support her work with the Earth, but also to anchor the energy of the higher rays into the one to seven rays of light.

Again we see the focus of embodiment. She creates a bridge of light between the higher vibrations of the spiritual realm and the Earth, which students on the Earth can access when connecting with the seventh ray to anchor a higher consciousness. With her loving energy she creates a seamless bond between the Earth, the planetary, solar and galactic levels of the spiritual hierarchy, to aid communication between all levels, and to integrate advanced wisdom and light into the Earth.

The workload and responsibilities she carries are immeasurable and unimaginable, but her efforts are for the beloved Creator and her brothers and sisters throughout the Earth and the Creator's universe. She sees every soul as her equal, wishing to help them in achieving their goals and lessons while on the Earth, and subsequently in the spiritual hierarchy. Every aspect of the spiritual ascension process is achievable, and Lady Quan Yin offers her energy to guarantee that each soul creates this as their reality.

Lady Quan Yin has a team of light workers assisting her in the eleventh ray ashram because of the great spiritual learning that can be achieved on this ray after the soul or monad merge. Some Pleiadians, Sirians and Andromedans work side by side within the eleventh ray ashram, as they see this ashram as an extension and combination of all the previous rays of light. Many Angels and Unicorns are attracted to work on the ray because of the great presence of love visible within the ashram.

The most dominant energy supporting the eleventh ray of light stems from the Great White Lodge, consisting of Ascended Masters who have evolved from the Earth and other realities. They wish to focus their energy and love onto the Earth to assist the souls in embodiment to achieve self-mastery and spiritual ascension. The white energy emitted from the female and male Ascended Masters of the Great White Lodge acts as an underlying support and boost for the eleventh ray energy.

Many of the Chohans of the previous rays are members of the Great White Lodge or Great White Brother and Sisterhood; they oversee the spiritual hierarchy especially at a planetary level. The Masters anchor their energy into every ray, offering their support in energising each one more strongly, but they have chosen to make their energy prominent in the eleventh ray ashram. It is here that students understand the process of mastery fully. If they haven't already mastered their being, bringing discipline to their mind, actions and emotions on the Earth and having ascended into the spiritual hierarchy, then it is on the eleventh ray that these preparations are instigated. Many lessons and examples are given on how to become a Master of the physical, emotional, mental and spiritual bodies.

The Masters working on this ray and the members of the Great White Lodge have already achieved mastery, so they make wonderful mentors to assist students in their final preparations and process of self-mastery. The anchoring of the Great White Lodge into the eleventh ray of light gives a new dimension to the ray: we may see it as a place of completion where one aspect of our spiritual evolution is coming to a close to begin a new spiritual quest.

Many of Lady Quan Yin's students are transported from her ashram to the Great White Lodge for greater learning. Students can even accompany a Master who is involved with their chosen spiritual career as a type of work experience, so they may gain a greater understanding of the spiritual hierarchy. This can sometimes happen during a person's sleep state if they are still manifested on the Earth, or as a form of tuition if they exist within their spiritual or light bodies or have travelled from another star within the Creator's universe.

Another reason the Ascended Masters chose the eleventh ray of light as a point to anchor their energy is because of the bridge of light created by Lady Quan Yin between Mother Earth and the many levels within the spiritual hierarchy. This bridge of light allows their energy to integrate with much of the spiritual hierarchy through the eleventh ray and its work in the spiritual world.

The eleventh ray holds many possibilities. We can invoke Lady Quan Yin and her eleventh ray to assist us if we are accelerating towards a soul or monad merge at a planetary level, if we wish to become more integrated with our souls, if we have achieved a soul or monad merge, wish to gain assistance with meditation and inner peace, wish to anchor greater love into our beings and receive healing, wish to resolve the karmic issues of our past or wish to embody and anchor the light of the Creator. We can imagine her energy flowing into our beings as we invoke her to assist us in our spiritual practices, to protect us and to connect us with the Great White Lodge and the Ascended Masters that will help us in our spiritual evolution. We may repeat her name in our minds as a mantra to truly feel the intensity of her loving powerful soul.

Allow Quan Yin to assist you in living a life of love, embodiment and peace on the Earth.

CHAPTER 26

LADY PALLAS ATHENA AND THE TWELFTH RAY OF LIGHT

Pallas Athena is known as a Greek Warrior Goddess because of her past lifetimes on the Earth. She appears to us in the spiritual realms as an expansive and blazing flame of golden light. She anchors the energy of the Christ Consciousness into her being with the power to burn up any negative energy, replacing it with the purity of the Creator. Her heart and soul are devoted to the energy of the Creator; she acts as a divine vessel of the Creator's light. She wholeheartedly surrenders her soul to the magnificence of the Creator, giving her the appearance of being strong, powerful and a great warrior of the light.

We on the Earth sometimes believe that surrendering ourselves to the divine energy of the Creator is to give our power away or to show ourselves as weak. Pallas Athena's gesture of surrendering to the Creator is courageous and allows her to work closely with the Creator and the Christ; they can see the energy of the mighty source emanating from her every action. Pallas Athena has been described as an Angel because of the sheer magnificence, tenderness, love and devotion she holds within her being. She shimmers with the golden energy of the Christ.

Pallas Athena is an Ascended Master and a Goddess; she is participating in anchoring the Goddess energy into the Earth to bring forth the balance between the male and female energies, while also working on the Board of Karma to eliminate the power of fear and the ego in the world.

Pallas Athena sends a beam of light from her soul to whoever calls on her assistance. This beam of golden light holds the divine love of the Creator within its energy and instantly burns up any negativity or karmic issues, replacing them with the high vibrational energy of the Christ. Pallas Athena is kind, gentle and caring to every soul manifestation of the Creator on the Earth, but when we invoke her to assist us she will take control of the situation with authority and power. Consequently, only love can be the result of any problems or experiences we have. Pallas Athena can find the core of any karmic issue or negative situation in our lives, quickly bringing it to our attention so it may be resolved, allowing us to move onward once more.

Her energy is so powerful and intense because as Chohan of the twelfth ray of light she has become an aspect of the Christ, due to its constant presence within her being. Pallas Athena teaches us that we can become complete embodiments of the Christ energy at a planetary level, if we allow her to assist us and invoke the energy of the twelfth ray of light to anchor into our beings.

One of the purest and highest rays of light available to us on a planetary level, the twelfth ray of light is of a shimmering golden colour. It is a port or sacred ashram where the energy of the Christ from the Christ Ashram and Lord Maitreya is anchored. The golden energy descends directly from the Creator's soul, through the Universal Logos, the Galactic Logos, the Solar Logos, Lord Buddha and Lord Maitreya, finally channelling into the twelfth ray of light. Pallas Athena continues the flow of golden energy by channelling it into all eleven rays of light at a planetary level.

In truth, this is one of the reasons for the presence of the Christ Consciousness as a ray of light: it is to anchor the Christ energy into the rays at a deeper level. The golden energy of the Christ flows through and integrates with each ray to ensure the purest form of love is evident and active in the rays, while also gathering the energy of all the rays so they may be united on the twelfth ray.

Pallas Athena wishes everyone to understand that the energy of the Christ exists within every soul; it runs through our bodies, our energy systems, and surrounds us constantly as we go about our daily routines. It is an invisible energy to those who are unable to see the energy of the Creator around them, but it is an immense and powerful energy, as it is the love of the Creator. The energy of the Christ Consciousness is evident within every kind, generous and loving gesture, action or expression that we make. When we anchor the Christ Consciousness into our beings and souls the golden energy enhances the love already existing within us, bringing it forth to be a greater influence in our lives, realities and actions. The energy of the Christ is the essence of our beings; it raises us to higher vibrations, new levels of consciousness, and assists us in fully realising the Christ or love consciousness within our beings and every soul throughout the universe.

Within Pallas Athena's ashram is a high vibrational energy of the Christ, but it is also a safe energy of the Creator's love that we can invoke, anchor and embody without harming our physical or light bodies. The energy anchored from the Creator into the Christ Ashram by Lord Maitreya is of a slightly higher vibration but still remains a safe energy for students working with and anchoring the energies of the planetary level. Archangel Metatron and Avatar Sai Baba are Cosmic Christs, but the Creator holds the highest vibration of love in our universe. As we evolve through our ascension processes, our constant mission will be to anchor, realise and express ever higher vibrations of the Christ Consciousness within our beings. Within the twelfth ray ashram there are several layers or levels of the Christ Consciousness, making it accessible to whoever invokes this divine energy.

It is the initiates who have completed their soul merge, and maybe even their ascension from the Earth, who can connect with the highest vibration of light available in the twelfth ray ashram. Many souls visit the twelfth ray from the Earth; numerous Masters also reside or work with the Christ ray of light to assist them in ascending to a solar level, or anchoring the next rays of light at this level into their beings.

The twelfth ray is a magnificent place as not only does it have students from Earth but also Ascended Masters, Star People and Extraterrestrials visiting its ashram to bathe in the Christ light. Many flock to visit and experience the Christ Absorption Chambers which rest within Pallas Athena's ashram. They are vast chambers within which the student or Master can sit, as golden shimmering energy of the Christ is poured into and around them, melting into every aspect of their being and soul. It is a wonderful experience that can increase the amount of love and awaken the Christ energy or love expression and actions within our beings.

We can all ask to visit the Christ Absorption Chambers to receive a shower of golden light from the twelfth ray of light during meditation. It is a cleansing and healing process and a form of uplift and rejuvenation. Many Masters enter the Christ Absorption Chambers as preparation before ascending to the next level of their consciousness and awareness, or prior to taking up their new role in the solar hierarchy. It is also a process that assists the merging of the soul at any level and continues to stabilise the presence of the soul within the physical or light body, if the individual has evolved from the tenth ray soul integration. We can, of course, visit the Christ Absorption Chamber whenever we want to. We first must invoke the twelfth ray of light and Pallas Athena to assist us as we ask to visit the chamber.

Pallas Athena in the twelfth ray ashram continues the work of Lady Quan Yin with students who are ascending through their soul expansion lessons with the assistance of the rays of light. After the students have passed through the eleventh ray of light and have anchored greater wisdom into their being with the support of the Great White Lodge Masters, Pallas Athena begins the process of complete integration with the Christ Consciousness at a planetary level.

The twelfth ray of light is an ashram that focuses on fully explaining the energy of the Christ and how we can use it to energise the power of the soul. It is because of its mission of educating and creating a new understanding of the Christ love energy that we are allowed to visit this ashram during our sleep states and meditations to anchor the energy into our beings whenever we wish to; the twelfth ray of light is accessible to anyone on the Earth.

Pallas Athena helps students to understand the vast energy and presence of love within their beings and the unity that they have with the Creator. It is an astonishing ray where the magnificence of the soul is absolutely and truly evident after the process of growth, acceptance and embodiment that has been completed. Students finally see themselves as beacons of the Creator's light and are able to expand their energy from their soul without limits.

The students that grasp, accept and absorb the highest vibration of the twelfth ray and Christ Consciousness are sent to Lord Maitreya by Pallas Athena to study and experience further the Christ energy of love. These students and souls discover how the Christ Lord Maitreya assists the Earth; they also integrate with his energy so they may assist the Earth and its inhabitants in embodying love.

Students who no longer reside on the Earth, but exist in their light bodies and are pursuing further studies with the twelfth ray with full conscious awareness, are most likely to visit the Christ Ashram. When their tuition is complete, Lord Maitreya will place the most suited Masters on the second ray of light and in the Synthesis Ashram, as these are smaller versions of the Christ Ashram and work directly with humanity on the Earth.

Wherever the Masters are placed they continue to learn about the

Christ Consciousness and the twelfth ray of light by working with the visiting students. Later they will return to the twelfth ray of light and continue their journey into the solar hierarchy for greater enlightenment. This is the path that some souls take when anchoring the twelfth ray of light, but obviously not all, as the twelfth ray of light offers much wisdom, spiritual education and a variety of paths in its loving ashram. Subsequently the Masters and students visiting the second ray of light can be transported to the twelfth ray of light to continue their understanding of the love of the Creator.

Lord Maitreya, Lord Melchizedek and Archangel Metatron are particularly active in their influence over the twelfth ray of light. Pallas Athena occasionally sends some of her students for visits to the universal level to inspire the higher vibrations of the Christ Consciousness within them, which assists her in anchoring the concentrated energy of the Christ into her ashram.

The twelfth ray of light is evidently a focal point for the spiritual hierarchy as it both assists souls at the beginning of their growth in awakening to the truth of their being, and souls drawing to the end of the lessons the planetary level has to offer. Not only is it a place of learning and of love, but it is a sacred place where souls become fully integrated with the Christ energy at a planetary level. The twelfth ray of light helps the second ray Masters and Chohans, Lord Maitreya and Lord Buddha, with bringing the energy of the Christ to the Earth. This process has been named 'the return of the Christ' or 'the anchoring of the new age of the Christ'. It represents the anchoring of greater love onto the Earth, allowing the entire civilisation to exist as manifestations of the Creator's pure love.

The Masters connected to the Christ Consciousness are continuing to pour the golden energy into the heart and essence of Mother Earth and her inhabitants to create a new generation where love, peace, harmony, and a faith and unity with the Creator triumph. By understanding this important information and the focus of the Masters, we can comprehend how essential it is for us to open our hearts and souls to the energy of the Christ and allow this divine golden light to run through our bodies, minds, actions and realities every second of the day. In following Pallas Athena's example and surrendering to the light of the Christ Consciousness, acknowledging its presence within our souls and the souls of others, we will assist ourselves to evolve and ascend closer to the source of the Creator.

The Mahatma, the Avatar of Synthesis known as the Cosmic Logos, is the energy supporting and integrating into the twelfth ray ashram. 'Mahatma' means 'great soul'. Its light is the highest energy available to the Earth and consists of three hundred and fifty-two layers of the Creator's energy.

The main focus of the Mahatma is to bring souls home to the soul of the Creator. Taking on numerous colours throughout the many dimensions of the spiritual hierarchy, the Mahatma energy appears as a soft turquoise energy at a physical level. The Mahatma acts as a support network for the twelfth ray and the Christ Consciousness, but it is also a neutral ground where a connection with the energy of the Mahatma can be made by students on the Earth, overseen by Pallas Athena. This is an appropriate ray for the Cosmic Logos to anchor its energy into, as both rays focus on integrating the Creator's energy. The vast consciousness of Mahatma fuses and bonds the divine energy of the Creator from the cosmic level with the light body students ascending through the levels of the spiritual hierarchy.

Mahatma assists students working with the twelfth ray of light to integrate and anchor the Christ Consciousness into their being; it is comparable to a gel bonding the soul and the Christ energy together. Mahatma also maintains the high vibration of the twelfth ray ashram, as the twelfth ray assists in anchoring the cosmic energy of the Mahatma into the Earth. The Mahatma offers greater wisdom to souls as they move forth to the solar level of the hierarchy, bestowing encouragement and a boost in their energy to assist them in their spiritual development journey and roles within the spiritual hierarchy. The Mahatma's function is akin to the presence of a manager or a high priest working on a lower level to reveal greater wisdom and enlightenment, inspiring souls to continue to devote their efforts and energy to the light of the Creator.

Pallas Athena receives a great volume of energy from the Mahatma or Cosmic Logos, assisting her with her mission of distributing and dispersing the energy of the Christ. This is one of the reasons her soul is so luminous and blazes so brightly. The Mahatma is the underlying thread anchoring into all rays of light, but most notably the twelfth ray.

If you feel a resonance with the cosmic energy of Mahatma then you can ask Pallas Athena to assist you in integrating this energy into your being, either during meditation or your sleep state. To transform the Earth we can constantly invoke Pallas Athena to anchor the Christ Consciousness into our beings, into Earth's inhabitants and the soul of Mother Earth.

Invoke Pallas Athena to assist you in realising the manifestation of the Creator's love within your physical body.

'I am Love.'

CHAPTER 27

AN INSIGHT INTO CONNECTING WITH THE RAYS

Making a connection, anchoring and integrating the energy of the rays of light individually and as a whole is a mission we should all hold close to our hearts. The rays act as a guiding light, assisting us in mastering our beings and expanding our spiritual awareness.

Each ray holds a particular quality that when embodied assists us in achieving mastery. The rays are available for us to invoke whenever we need support and assistance in our lives, but they exceed this: they are a manual, a teaching process that allows us to grasp our lessons of spiritual growth on the Earth.

Each Chohan of the rays acts as a spiritual mentor and helps us to integrate different aspects of the mighty Creator's soul into our beings while on the Earth, and even when in the spiritual world. By invoking the different rays of light and interlacing them into our actions on the Earth, we can and will achieve a tremendous growth process that brings new enlightenment and a sense or unity with the spiritual hierarchy and the Creator.

We must remember that our ultimate goal is to understand the rays of light in our own way, to enact their sacred qualities within every moment of our realities, and to unite all rays of light within our soul and entire being as an absolute presence. With this in mind it is essential to invoke rays that we feel a connection with or a need to experience, to explore their meaning to us as individuals. It is through experiencing the rays that we will obtain complete integration with the twelve energies and consciousness of the Creator.

We can begin by focusing our energies on the first three rays of light. Anchoring the divine plan, will, love, wisdom and manifestation skills of the Creator will help us to gain an initial understanding of the rays, which will springboard us forward on our paths of growth. Just by focusing on these rays each day we can evolve to a higher level of spiritual growth with the guidance of the Chohans.

The energy of the fourth and sixth rays adds greater depth to our process of evolution, allowing us to connect with the beauty of the Creator manifest in every aspect of our lives, and to increase our inner faith.

The seventh ray of light is the key to awakening a new level of consciousness within our beings, removing fear to allow expansion to occur.

The fifth ray of light assists us in connecting and understanding the divine soul within our beings, while the rays eight, nine and ten focus on developing the presence of the soul or monad and the light body within the physical body.

The eleventh and twelfth rays of light enhance the completion of the soul or monad merge at a planetary level, and anchor the purest form of love from the Christ into the individual to assist in further development.

When we view the rays together, we understand that we can access and anchor into our minds an educational program direct from the spiritual planes.

While discussing the rays with Master Kuthumi, he revealed a valuable piece of information that can assist us in continuing to anchor the energy of each ray deeper into our beings. Each ray has many aspects and levels to its energy, and when we invoke a ray of light we only connect with one level of the ray. For example, if we invoke the second ray of light without specifying which level of the second ray we wish to access, we will receive the lowest level of blue energy. Each time we invoke the second ray light throughout the day only focusing on this energy and no other, we would continue to receive the same energy level. We would form a connection with the second ray, but this bond would not develop, despite our continuous efforts to channel the energy into our beings.

We can combat this by asking to receive the highest energy vibration available to our beings from the second ray of light to anchor into our bodies; this will ensure that when we invoke the second ray of light we receive the correct level of light and energy for our own spiritual growth process. Understanding this can be helpful when beginning to connect with the rays, as it stabilises the energy within our bodies. The problem is that when we focus only on the second ray of light throughout the day, we will only ever receive the level of light energy we anchored into our beings with the first invocation.

Master Kuthumi's divine key for connection with the rays, so as to ensure we continue to anchor new levels of light, is to invoke the rays alternately. First we invoke the second ray of light, then half an hour later we invoke the third ray of light. When we invoke the second ray again, we will actually receive a fraction higher energy vibration from it because we changed the flow of energy entering into our beings. We might spend a whole day invoking the second ray of light, and the next day invoking the first ray of light. If we invoke the second ray again on the third day, we will receive a higher vibration of energy than we did when we first invoked the second ray. The key is to focus on invoking a variety of rays throughout the day. Even if you only choose two rays to invoke in one day, as you alternate between them you will gain a deeper anchoring of each.

We receive a higher vibration of energy each time we re-anchor a ray of light into our beings because the flow has been broken. The ray or Chohan senses we have already obtained a certain level of the ray's energy within our beings, and so they intensify the energy to assist our mission of integrating with the rays. When we only invoke one ray, the light simply flows continuously through our bodies without progression and can become stagnant. Master Kuthumi guides and encourages us to anchor more than one ray of light during the day because the rays are united and work together; the presence of more than one ray will allow them to enhance each other's energy.

We can invoke Master Kuthumi to explain his insight concerning the rays of light in further detail if we need to. He is always available to bestow new wisdom and inspirations on souls incarnate on the Earth.

To begin our integration with the rays of light, we can first determine the qualities we would believe to be beneficial within our reality to aid our goals and to manifest our desires. This is a process of evaluating your own character to determine how you can improve yourself, then looking towards the rays of light to anchor necessary energies or qualities into your being.

Another method of beginning your embodiment of the rays of light is to discover which ones your soul, monad and the Creator have already anchored into your being. This requires a simple meditation, calling upon your guides to surround you in their love and protection, while invoking the assistance and guidance of the Manu Allah Gobi, the Christ Lord Maitreya, the Mahachohan Saint Germain and the Divine Director of the Rays. While holding the intention of comprehending the rays of light anchored into your entire being, keep this focus for a while, and then ask to be made aware of the ray or rays of light currently anchored into your physical body. You may sense, see or simply accept a number from one to twelve.

You can continue this process, asking to discover the ray or rays of light anchored into your etheric body, emotional body, mental body, spiritual body, soul and monad. This may require practice as you will have to become accustomed to the format in which you receive this knowledge. But with this additional information you have a template to work from and can concentrate on anchoring the particular rays of light you have discovered you need into each specified energy body every day. It is important to realise that even though the rays of light are anchored into our entire being, they do not truly become active or influential until we begin to work with them.

An additional and interesting practice is to apply the above technique with the intention of discovering the ray of light that is most *needed* within each aspect of your being. You may gain diverse results, but it can help to compare the rays of light anchored with the rays that are needed, offering a goal of achievement. Discovering the rays of light that you already hold and the rays that are needed assists you in evaluating your energy further, and discerning the rays most essential for your spiritual advancement.

It is important to review the rays of light anchored into your entire being every few months as this will aid a steady progression of integration and exploration of the rays of the Creator's soul. Your purpose can become evident through your analysis of the rays linked with your energy bodies, soul and monad.

PART 3

BEYOND THE PLANETARY LEVEL

CHAPTER 28

THE HIGHER MANIFESTATIONS OF
THE SPIRITUAL HIERARCHY

This chapter is mostly for the purpose of enlightenment, helping us to gain a greater comprehension of the goals we have to achieve in order to return and become truly united with the Creator.

The high vibrational energies are not as accessible to people on the Earth as the planetary energies, but we can occasionally invoke them for support in our growth. Most people when invoking the higher frequencies will only receive planetary level energies as their guides protectively ignore their request, supplementing them instead with lower vibrations. Our guides understand that in order for us to access these higher levels of the Creator's universe, we must first completely comprehend and integrate with the planetary level.

The ideas and insights in this chapter are therefore simply to expand our awareness, helping us to see that there is life and growth beyond the planetary level and the Earth. The lower energies of the solar level are an exception and are available to us as they merge and integrate into the planetary level. Allow the preceding information to spark within you the desire and passion to follow your spiritual path, inspiring you to focus on your current path within the planetary level of the hierarchy, later to embark on a journey of discovery into the universe of the Creator.

The solar level of the hierarchy is headed by the Solar Logos, Helios and Vesta. They are a masculine and feminine energy working as a combined soul to oversee the solar level and influence the planetary level with the energy they anchor. From the Solar Logos Ashram they emanate a copper golden colour of light to signify their position in the universe; they are Masters of our Solar System. The solar light is of a higher or quicker vibration than the white light of the Planetary Logos, it acts as a vibrant sun within the universe that specialises in activation, energising and bringing forth in a fiery energy and colour the warmth and tenderness of the core love of the Creator.

Helios and Vesta anchor many aspects of the Creator into their combined soul. They have integrated their masculine and feminine energies together in harmony working as a whole, while still recognising their individual aspects and personalities. They exist as a vibrant, blazing luminous soul of the Creator's light. The radiance of their energy is awe-inspiring and they act as vessels of the Creator's light, allowing many to bathe in their divine energies. Within the spiritual hierarchy they are most definitely beacons of light; they are one of the brightest lights we can invoke safely from the Earth.

Helios and Vesta exist as a unity of the brightest sunlight we can imagine. They use their light as their power and tool to aid the solar level, resulting in all Masters working within their level inhabiting a great luminosity. It is a prominent mission of the solar level to anchor and absorb greater light, accepting the sunny rays emanating from the Solar Logos Ashram. The light of each Master or student connecting or present within this energy will be amplified and enhanced to prepare them for integrating into the galactic level of the hierarchy and the teachings presented.

Both Helios and Vesta are very active and involved in the solar level; their energy embodies and surrounds this level with great intensity. They hold strong influences within the planetary level, overseeing the general work and missions of our Planetary Logos Lord Buddha and his team, while sharing their wealth of wisdom and supportive energy. Their energy naturally integrates into the high vibrations of the planetary level, but with the permission of the Creator and Lord Buddha they have taken a greater interest in our spiritual practices and development. They offer a special service to all who feel a resonance with their energy or wish to increase the luminosity of their soul.

We are permitted to invoke Helios and Vesta once during our day on the Earth to anchor their solar energy into our beings and souls. We may ask them to activate our souls and energy systems at a planetary level, to pour their copper golden light into our beings to raise our energy vibrations and, most importantly, increase our light quotients. If we are ready to receive this energy surge we will experience a major transformation and uplift by the simple invocation. If the timing is not exactly appropriate, then their light will anchor into our souls on a smaller scale until we are ready to work with them. This is a special privilege we can all take advantage of, as long as we ask to receive the perfect amount of energy for our beings and are respectful of the high vibrations associated with these beings of light.

'I invoke the Solar Logos, Helios and Vesta to kindly pour, anchor and channel the perfect amount of your vibrant and luminous solar energy into my being. Allow your light to support my current spiritual progresses, activating the light of my planetary soul and raising my energy vibrations. Let me feel the love of your sunny light within my being, creating a process of rejuvenation. Help me to become a beacon as dazzling as you, on the Earth.'

Once we have harmonised with the planetary level and twelve rays of light, Helios and Vesta will aid us in anchoring our solar light bodies into our beings to raise our vibrations in unity with the solar level. This mustn't be attempted unless we have first asked Lord Buddha to anchor our planetary light body into our physical body, working with him for a significant amount of time. Invoking the solar light body before anchoring our planetary light body can cause imbalance. Helios and Vesta aid their solar students in anchoring their solar chakras, soul aspects, light quotient, energy vibration and solar luminosity into their beings.

It must be repeated that we are permitted to anchor and invoke the light of the Solar Logos into our lives when necessary to boost our energies, but not to begin integration with this level before the planetary level. Helios and Vesta make themselves available to all, as the students of the Earth are raising their energy vibration and awareness. The Solar Logos wishes to act in offering teachings and divine examples of the luminosity that can be gained by us on the Earth.

Within the copper golden solar vibration of light are the twelve rays of light. These come forth from the Galactic Logos and are distributed into the solar level. Within the Solar Logos Ashram are the prominent energies of the first three rays of light at a higher vibration, expressing the core qualities of the Creator. The two last rays of light, eleven and twelve, are also anchoring the Solar and Galactic Christ and integrate the solar level with Masters at this vibration.

The solar level is comprised of many levels of growth and development for a Master to evolve through. Masters or students aim to obtain a position within the solar level schooling so that they may absorb and anchor the copper golden vibration, the solar twelve rays of light and the Solar Christ into their beings. A new solar Master may occupy a role within the departments of the solar level or may anchor the energies while existing at a different level within the hierarchy or on a planet within the Creator's universe. The students of the solar level must be aligned with the solar level for certain amounts of time to gain complete luminosity and to study under the resident Masters. Most of us on the Earth exist within the planetary level with a planetary consciousness; with development we can exist on the Earth with a solar consciousness. It is similar for the solar Masters and light beings; they can either inhabit the solar level or exist at a planetary level. Some exist at a solar level while anchoring the galactic level.

The boundaries between each level are limitless as we progress up the spiritual ladder or anchor the energies into our beings. The divisions described between each of the five higher aspects of the hierarchy are to aid our comprehension *(see diagram, page 14)*. In truth, the levels integrate and merge together seamlessly, as do the solar and planetary twelve rays of light. They are united as the whole of the Creator's soul. This allows souls progressing from the planetary level gradually to become accustomed to the higher vibrations of the solar level, and so forth. The departments that we see in the planetary level and to some extent the solar level are to assist our comprehension, but they are also influenced by the physicality of the Earth, which divides aspects of the Creator into accessible energies.

There are twelve departments or ashrams dedicated to the solar twelve rays of light. Each has its own Chohan and team of assistants. Some Chohans of the planetary level progress to occupy or command a different ray of light in the solar level, to expand and broaden their understanding of the Creator's energy. Uniting with the solar twelve rays of light promotes a clear and in depth understanding of the rays and their qualities, thus comprehending and harmonising with the Creator. The twelve solar rays plunge the soul into greater discovery of its own energies, abilities and inner presence. All qualities and teachings connected to the rays are heightened beyond the planetary level to allow accelerated growth to occur.

The colours of the solar rays are slightly paler than our planetary rays. We are able to detect our planetary rays by colour, but at a solar level we learn to distinguish them by their vibration or frequency, heightening our senses. When we detect the rays consciously we realise that colour is not important but is simply an expression of our understanding of the ray. Although the rays of light are paler at a solar level, we must also open our mind to the idea that a paler version of a colour on the Earth may manifest as a completely different colour at a solar level. For example, the red of the first ray may manifest as a pale blue or golden colour at a solar level. We must realise that the knowledge we hold now about our reality doesn't always marry with the realities of the higher levels of the Creator's universe.

There is a Solar Manu overseeing the solar first ray department, working closely with our Manu Allah Gobi. The Solar Christ named as Abraham oversees the second ray, while receiving the Christ energy from the Galactic Christ and distributing it to Lord Maitreya. Abraham is a name this soul has chosen, not because of past lifetimes, but due to the vibration of the name. We can invoke the energy of the Solar Christ Abraham to integrate into our beings alongside the energy of the Planetary Christ.

The Solar Mahachohan carries similar responsibilities to our Master Saint Germain, overseeing the solar rays three to seven. A Solar Divine Director of Rays exists within the team assisting the Solar Logos Helios and Vesta. Solar Teachers also reside within this level of the hierarchy to aid Masters and students who have developed through the planetary level to realise and adjust to the solar vibration, anchoring its educational processes.

The planetary and solar levels demonstrate vibrant colours of the rays because they are involved in the creation of the Earth and exist closer to its physical and heavy vibrations. As we evolve up the hierarchy of levels, the colours of the twelve rays become clear and translucent and the divisions between the levels are almost nonexistent, their unity and wholeness apparent. When we delve into these higher levels we will see the departments are comparable to those of the planetary level, but they appear seamless to us on the Earth, making it difficult for us to separate and even comprehend them. Many souls travel and enrol themselves in the Earth's unique schooling so they may experience the twelve rays of the Creator's sacred soul in physical low vibrational forms, seeing the vivid colours and learning to truly secure the qualities of the Creator into their being. Enrolling in the Earth's schooling means they will be able to move through all vibrations of the twelve rays of light within the Creator's universe, perceiving the twelve rays of light at their varying vibrations.

Overseeing the mission of Helios and Vesta and governing the purpose of the galactic level is the Galactic Logos Melchior, so named in celebration of the full integration of the masculine and feminine energies to create one soul. Unlike Helios and Vesta, who are a masculine and feminine aspect combined but still holding their individual names, Melchior is the name created when a full integration of both aspects was achieved. This symbolises the vibration and awareness of growth and spiritual development inhabiting the galactic level of the hierarchy. We each have a feminine and masculine aspect within us, but in order to achieve complete integration we must realise both energies in harmony. Sometimes the opposite aspect to our current gender can materialise in physical or light body form to aid our acceptance.

Melchior is powerful, loving, inspirational, and a high vibrational soul energy, overseeing and embodying the Earth's galaxy. When we invoke the Galactic Logos to connect with us and pour the galactic divine energy into our beings, it can be extremely intense, as it runs throughout our bodies, causing a lethargic or sleepy sensation. This is because the physical body has difficulty incorporating the fine and vast light. The greater volume of planetary light we anchor into our beings, the more able we are to accept the energy direct from the galactic level. Absorbing the energy of the Galactic Logos free from stress can only be achieved by progressing through the layers and levels of the lower spiritual hierarchy to gain a foundation of understanding and vibration.

This said, we are able to access the galactic light by asking for it to be channelled through the Solar Logos Helios and Vesta, then through the Planetary Logos Lord Buddha and eventually through an Ascended Master of our choice. Master Kuthumi, Manu, Christ or Mahachohan would be excellent choices as they are accustomed to these high vibrational energies. The result is that we receive the perfect vibration and frequency of energy and light for our beings without putting any unneeded stress on our physical bodies. This system can be used to connect with all the higher levels of the spiritual hierarchy and can be applied when linking with an Ascended Master, if you are sensitive to their intense energy.

Invoking the galactic energy on occasions can aid in integrating the planetary and solar levels at a greater depth; both are unified in their entirety into the Galactic Logos. The Galactic Logos has much wisdom to share with humanity; viewing our planet from a distance, Melchior is able to offer new wisdom that others may not be able to see because of their attachment to the Earth. Melchior is a spiritual mentor who instils discipline and focus into students while demonstrating the expansive and limitless energy and aspect of their being. Intense and profound learning is achieved at the galactic level as all Masters existing within this level study personally with Melchior. Much wisdom is downloaded from the universal and multi-universal levels into the galactic level to assist the growth of the Masters in the lower aspects of the hierarchy and the inhabitants of the Earth.

The ray of light extending from the Galactic Logos Ashram is of a silver golden colour. This energy is present within the lower spiritual hierarchy and in smaller fractions on the Earth. Still the energy of the Christ Consciousness is integrated into this level and supports the Christ at a planetary level, downloading information and additional vibrations for Lord Maitreya to access. The silver light can be invoked on the Earth as a protective energy to surround us in a shield against negative energy.

Within the galactic level are the galactic twelve rays of light, their Chohans and teams of light workers. The teachings of the galactic twelve rays are currently focused on the complete expression of the soul as a vast individual, an integrated aspect of the galactic level and team as well as of the Creator.

On the planetary level we experiment within the twelve rays of light with many spiritual practices and training exercises that are studied in depth on the higher levels. The solar level and the solar twelve rays focus on illumination of every aspect of our beings, while the galactic level and galactic twelve rays focus on the integration of the masculine and feminine aspects, integration with the Creator and the Earth's galaxy. Realising and accepting our powers is the essence of the galactic level. The galactic twelve rays of light assist in the integration of the galactic light body, soul aspect, chakras, sun or luminosity, light quotient and energy vibration. A bridge or connection of light is built between the student or soul and the galactic level, which incorporates all previous levels. This process of integration is integrated into the education of the twelve rays of light at all levels of the hierarchy. The twelve rays of light at each level of the spiritual hierarchy exist as guides and paths to aid integration with each level of growth, development and unity.

The energy vibrations of the universal level are beyond the galactic level and yet it is this level that many of us can connect with without feeling the stress and pressure of the intense energy. This is due to the resident Universal Logos, Lord Melchizedek and his active presence in the Earth's evolution. 'Melchizedek' is a title given to enlightened initiates of the Order of Melchizedek who have discovered and enhanced their divine connection with the Creator. The Order of Melchizedek during Atlantean and ancient Egyptian times was known as a spiritual mystery school at which many incarnate Ascended Masters trained while on the Earth. The title of Melchizedek describes our Universal Logos as an integrated and wise soul of high vibrations governing the Earth's universe. Lord Melchizedek can appear as a beautiful white and golden light Christ, whose generosity and desire to aid humanity manifests as a wealth of love pouring from his soul.

He is continually evolving, currently integrating and anchoring his energies into the multi-universal level; Melchizedek is in mid transition of becoming the new Multi-Universal Logos. This is a gradual process as there is much for Lord Melchizedek to accept and comprehend. Governing the multi-universal level is a major responsibility, as the Logos must oversee the multi-universal level and all levels, Masters and light beings prior to this.

The Multi-Universal Logos holds a great influence in the progress of the Earth and its inhabitants, ensuring that all Masters and incarnate souls receive the correct version, instructions and divine will of the Creator's plan for the Earth's universe. Lord Melchizedek is slowly integrating into the position of the multi-universal level while training a Master to take his position as Universal Logos. Any problems that occur at these high vibrational frequencies can cause traumatic and drastic effects to the entire spiritual hierarchy, as everything proceeds down through these high levels and the Creator's mighty soul. Lord Melchizedek must constantly focus his mind and thoughts positively.

This may be a natural habit at this stage of growth, but we must remember that a small fraction of the ego is ever present. A single negative thought could lower the entire vibration of the hierarchy and the Earth. With this insight we can comprehend the purpose of our planetary Masters reminding us to lovingly control our minds and thoughts, dissolving the fear and negativity of the ego. The higher our vibration evolves, the more our thoughts affect our reality and the realities of others. It is because of this that Lord Melchizedek's transition is gradual, so as not to upset the balance of the hierarchy.

Lord Melchizedek works with Lord or Archangel Metatron, who is a Cosmic Christ, leader of all Archangels and the angelic kingdom. Archangel Metatron is among smaller numbers of souls who have lived on the Earth in a physical body, later evolving to follow the path of an Archangel. He now inhabits the multi-universal level, currently aiding and activating Lord Melchizedek's growth while acting as a major overseer of the multi-universal level. The current Multi-Universal Logos is not so accessible; it is through Archangel Metatron that we can comprehend the energy.

The ray of light extending from the universal level and Lord Melchizedek's ashram is of a golden colour. It is the purity of the Christ Consciousness, existing at a vastly higher vibration and frequency than the planetary golden energy. It is at this stage that we see the last vibrant colour of the Christ Consciousness – in the higher levels it is of a clear colour. The Planetary Christ Ashram holds a deep connection with the universal level; both hold a Christ Ashram, with the Universal Ashram fuelling the Planetary Ashram.

The bond between Lord Maitreya and Lord Melchizedek is unbreakable; they frequently converse telepathically with each other. They unite in the passion to anchor the Christ Consciousness or essence of love from the core soul of the Creator into the Earth.

This could be one of the reasons for Lord Melchizedek's accessibility to humankind on the Earth. The acceptance and realisation of the solar and galactic levels by us on the Earth is not as profound as the acceptance of Lord Melchizedek. It seems anomalous that the Solar Christ, Abraham, is not as influential as the Universal Christ, but this may be due to Lord Melchizedek's exceptional ability to step down his energy and travel through the dimensions and energy vibrations of the spiritual hierarchy with great ease. When we anchor the golden energy of Lord Maitreya at a planetary level, we may also ask Lord Melchizedek to boost this energy vibration to integrate a fraction of the Universal Christ into our beings.

Another reason for our bond with Lord Melchizedek is his ability to anchor his energy into the many initiates of the Order of Melchizedek throughout the hierarchy, allowing us to become accustomed to his presence in many ways. These beings can be known as disciples of the Melchizedek Order, but there is also a group of souls known as the Melchizedek Disciples who exist in the Universal Logos Ashram as a supportive energy for Lord Melchizedek. They are the equivalent of Lord Buddha's Twelve Buddhas, acting as a council of guidance. It is one of the Melchizedek Disciples that will occupy the position of Universal Logos after Lord Melchizedek. In truth, the title of Melchizedek may for the foreseeable future govern the Universal

Logos position, as it is a name that many enlightened beings at this level possess.

We on the Earth may invoke the high vibration and illumined wisdom of the Melchizedek Disciples to develop our expansion and accelerate our spiritual growth as a supportive energy to complement the teachings of the planetary level. We must demonstrate respect of their energy at all times, their responsibilities are vast. They do not take kindly to humans invoking their energy under false pretences to gain additional power, but when we hold pure love within our hearts they will naturally be attracted to work with us.

The universal level and Logos is a point or bridge that connects the lower and higher aspects of the spiritual hierarchy together. It is through Lord Melchizedek that the higher energies of the Creator are channelled into the Masters in the planetary, solar and galactic levels of the hierarchy. These levels are able to connect with the higher levels of the hierarchy by accessing the energy from the Universal Logos. The universal level is a valuable tool for both the higher and lower levels and their Masters. Lord Melchizedek has had a wealth of experience in communicating with Masters and humans; he has truly mastered the art of reducing his energy vibration to a stable, acceptable frequency for all walks of life on a spiritual path. We are able to safely and securely invoke his energy as he will direct the perfect amount of light into our beings through the correct channels and paths.

The special golden ray of the universal level is contained within the Universal Ashram; here there are many chambers of growth, activation and integration that we can visit when we have harmonised with the planetary level. We are permitted to invoke Lord Melchizedek for healing with his golden energy, and amazingly, allowed to visit certain chambers within the universal chambers to develop our spiritual awareness, expansion and acceptance. These chambers have been especially set aside for humanity to visit during meditation or their sleep state. Again, if you are not ready to experience the golden healing chambers then this request may be ignored or supplanted by the planetary Christ energy. The energy of these few chambers is slightly lower in vibration, and it is our souls or light bodies that visit rather than our physical aspect. The energies are then filtered appropriately into the physical body and personality.

The universal twelve rays of light are not readily available to humanity as they denote a vast process of growth, integration and activation gained through the teachings of the solar and galactic twelve rays of light, enhanced by the universal twelve rays of light. We must remember that the qualities of the rays remain similar at whatever level we view them, but the teachings of the rays become limitless, with wisdom beyond our comprehension. A Master at this level would not access the rays individually but as one vast energy vibration and integrated beam of light, similar to a pale rainbow of the twelve colours surging into the soul. There still remain Chohans of the twelve universal rays, but these Chohans focus on many rays rather than governing one.

At the multi-universal level the twelve ray Chohans work with all rays of light, united as a governing body. Positions and titles are difficult to distinguish at these high vibrations: as all Masters work as one unity, labels and titles are not needed. They do not see themselves as separate departments or individuals, but as a harmonised team. The Masters or students are so evolved and integrated at this level of the hierarchy that they immediately take the position of Chohans of the rays to gain the utmost learning experience, rather than acting as students under resident Chohans. There are far fewer Masters within the higher levels compared to the planetary level, as many have united with their monads and soul extensions to become vast souls.

The multi-universal level exudes a platinum ray of light, while the cosmic level expresses a translucent energy. Both levels merge as one with each other and the Creator's vast soul. Divisions even between the levels are non-existent. Integration at this level is no longer a goal but an absolute and fully realised aspect of existence. The golden, platinum and translucent energies merge as one, with the translucent energy at the pinnacle point of the Creator's vibration.

The cosmic aspect of the spiritual hierarchy is a truly integrated extension of the Creator's mighty soul of fine vibrations. The Avatar of Synthesis, also named the Mahatma energy, holds the title of Cosmic Logos for the Earth and the Creator's universe. The Mahatma consists of three hundred and fifty-two levels of growth and vibration, which are present within the entire spiritual hierarchy at various vibrations. We can invoke the energy of the Mahatma to accelerate our spiritual evolution as we will connect with the perfect vibration within the vast Mahatma energy. The Mahatma assists with integration at all levels of the spiritual hierarchy.

The Cosmic Logos receives the plans and will of the Creator, with the responsibility of distributing them through the entire spiritual hierarchy. The twelve rays of light, now at their purest, clear form, are channelled into the Cosmic Logos and the Council of Twelve Cosmic Beings, who govern all Chohans and ray departments in the entire hierarchy. The twelve rays of light are united as a whole energy, but their separations are noted by the Council of Twelve, as they understand the lower departments within the hierarchy.

Within the cosmic level the love and Christ Consciousness of the Creator is in its purity, but there isn't a governing Christ, simply the Creator with many realised Ascended Masters or Avatars who have accepted themselves as a Cosmic Christ. This title is both the truth and symbolic: it represents their unity with the Creator and the many teachings, realisations and activations beyond which they have progressed. The Cosmic Christs or Beings are available for us to connect with as they lovingly continue to aid the development and evolution of the Earth. These Cosmic Beings may have experienced life on the Earth, but they have also visited and existed on many different planets, stars and dimensions within the Creator's universe. They are equipped to support us on our spiritual path, as they have walked the path before us.

The vast and limitless Creator from which we all extend is the pinnacle of the Earth spiritual hierarchy.

Many of us may crave to be united with the Creator, but see the spiritual hierarchy as a daunting ladder up which we must climb to great heights beyond our imagination. However, the Creator is in complete manifestation in the Cosmic Beings of the cosmic level, within Lord Melchizedek and his disciples. The Creator is present wholeheartedly within the galactic and solar levels, within all the Masters and light workers mentioned, and within the millions not named who share their precious and valuable light.

Most importantly for us, the Creator is in true manifestation in our planetary level, within the many Ascended Masters, Chohans and spiritual teachers whom we can call our friends and companions.

The Creator is united within Lord Buddha, our divine and respected leader and governor, who inspirationally lights his torch to lead us forth.

The divine and sacred energies of the Creator exist within our beings, within each and every physical body on the Earth.

The concept that the Creator exists within us, in full manifestation, is the purpose of the twelve rays of light. With this notion we can change the world, because we are united completely and wholeheartedly with the Creator. We do not need to seek or search for the Creator, but must simply realise we are the Creator in sacred manifestation on the Earth, and we have been granted the twelve rays of light to aid this discovery.

GLOSSARY

Angel
An Angel is a being of light created from the heart and love energy of the Creator. Angels act as messengers from the Creator to humanity and hold all loving qualities of the Creator for humanity to absorb and embody. We can call upon the Angels to assist us in all matters within our reality and spiritual growth as they will align us to the core and essential energy of the Creator.

Archangel
Archangels hold the same purpose as the Angels, but they also oversee the work and purpose of the Angelic Kingdom or community. They could be seen as the leaders and essential holders of important Creator energies and qualities for humanity to absorb and embody. Archangels are powerhouses of love that will divinely intervene in our realities when we ask and allow them to.

Ascended Master
An Ascended Master is a soul that has existed on the Earth and has realised him or herself as their truth and as the Creator. An Ascended Master has disciplined and brought into balance his or her emotions, thoughts and energy bodies, existing in harmony and peace with the Creator and all that is the Creator. Ascended Masters hold a great volume of knowledge and act as guides to humanity from the spiritual levels and planes. With the current changes that are occurring, more Ascended Masters are choosing to delay their ascension or return to the inner planes to assist humanity.

Ascension
Ascension is the process of self-realisation, soul realisation and Creator realisation. It is a period of growth where one focuses on aligning to the Creator's soul and becoming the Creator. Ascension is the journey

of evolvement that you walk from the moment of awakening to the moment of complete alignment with the Creator.

Ascension Seat
An Ascension Seat is an energy point on the inner planes which holds a certain focus. Whether it is healing or enlightenment, this seat is usually created by an Ascended Master to allow humanity to align with the energy to accelerate their spiritual growth or boost the volume of light they hold.

Ashram
Ashram is a sacred space which can be created on the Earth or inner planes where one can align to divine energies, and learn or practise specific teachings to aid growth.

Avatar
Avatar is a title given to one who truly realises themselves as the Creator, holding a higher percentage of Creator energies and qualities than an Ascended Master. Avatars can return to the Earth as an example to others or can continue to evolve and share their teachings from the inner planes.

Chakra
Chakras are energy points or wheels – vortices – within our body that hold and absorb the Creator's light; they maintain our perfect health and wellbeing on a spiritual and physical level by ensuring a constant flow of life force energy around the body.

Channel
A channel is like an invisible tube built into your crown chakra that extends into the heavens; the channel is built from light and allows light, energy and wisdom to enter into the human mind.

Chohan
Chohan is a title offered to Ascended Masters or beings of light that oversee and act as leaders of the rays of light and their departments. A Chohan completely embodies the ray of light he or she leads, acting as a teacher and example to others of integration with the aspect of the Creator present.

Christ
Christ refers to the loving heart energy of the Creator; it is the purest vibration of love. The Christ consciousness and Christ beings act as examples to all of how to exist both as love, and in love. We all hold the energy of the Christ within us and can all exist as a Christ being on the Earth.

Consciousness
Consciousness is a state of awareness, perception, understanding, realisation, knowledge and active presence.

Creator
'Creator' is one of the many names of God.

Elementals
Elementals are spirits and souls existing on an unseen level who devote their energy and purpose to caring for and nurturing the Earth, Nature Kingdoms and Mother Earth.

Fairy
Fairies are souls who devote their energy and purpose to working alongside nature and the animal kingdom in order to allow the Creator's energy to anchor, blossom and thrive. People who work closely with Mother Earth often have fairy guides, who are essentially pure loving beings of light holding ancient knowledge of how to exist as one with Mother Earth.

Goddess
A Goddess is a being of light who holds the feminine, nurturing and creative qualities, energy and wisdom of the Creator.

Guides
When using the term 'Guides', we are most often referring to those who assist us on an unseen level, supporting or inspiring our spiritual growth. We each have a special community of guides who surround us and assist us at certain times in our lives. These guides are most often beings with whom we have in the past held a strong connection, or who hold wisdom that is essential for our growth.

Inner Planes
Inner planes describes the unseen levels of energy beyond the Earth's physical and heavy vibration, the dimensions or heavens of the Creator, the space in which the Ascended Masters, Angels and all light beings exist.

Intuition
Everyone has the ability to use their intuition; it is the instinct, insight and knowing feeling within you that acts as a guiding light along your path. To follow your intuition is to follow your soul and Creator wisdom.

Light Beings
A Light Being is a soul, person, essence or energy that holds and emanates the light of the Creator.

Light Body
A light body is a sacred grid-work of light that anchors into our physical body with spiritual development to aid ascension. It houses our soul when we evolve from our physical existence, and when we travel to ashrams on the inner planes during our sleep states.

Light Quotient
'Light Quotient' refers to the volume or percentage of light or Creator energy that you hold within your mind and body.

Logos
'Logos' is a title given to a being that is the source of world order, or one who holds and understands the Creator's will. A Logos acts as an overseer to a level and vibration of the Creator's universe. We have six Logoi who act as examples of levels of Creator embodiment.

Meditation
Meditation is a practice that essentially encourages us to connect with the energy of peace and harmony within us, dissolving all thoughts and simply existing in the present, observing ourselves and our energies. Meditation disciplines the mind and creates a stillness that awakens the senses, thus creating or developing new spiritual connections.

Monad
'Monad' is another label for 'Soul Group'; it is a higher, more whole aspect of you. Your monad extends from the Creator. Many souls extend from your monad, and you are one of these extensions.

Mother Earth
Mother Earth is the essence and spirit of the Earth and the Nature Kingdom.

Ray
A ray is energy, light and sound vibration combined as one, holding the same quality or intention from the Creator's soul. A ray holds a wealth of knowledge and enlightenment from the Creator which we can absorb and process to aid our own spiritual growth. The vibration of a ray can be represented by a colour. A ray of light can be anchored into your body, energy and reality; we can also visit the inner plane anchoring point or department of each ray to become fully integrated.

Soul
The essence and truth of your being; the aspect, energy, light, love and knowledge within you that originally extended from the Creator's soul. Your soul is your Creator presence.

Spirit
The word spirit can often be used to depict a soul or the essence of a person; it can also be used to describe a person who exists without a physical body. The spirit of a person is their divine will, determination, intuition, creativity and strength, essentially their entire energy.

Unicorn
A being of pristine light of the same energy vibration as the Angelic Kingdom. Often seen as ascended horses, unicorns hold a powerful ability to aid and teach manifestation, as well as creating miracles in your reality. They are powerful healers holding the energy of purity.

SUMMARY OF THE TWELVE RAYS, THEIR CHOHANS AND QUALITIES

Ray	Colour	Chohan	Qualities	Purpose
1st	Red	Master El Morya	Divine Will and Plan of the Creator, Power, Courage, Determination, Action	Enacting & Existing as the Will of the Creator
2nd	Blue	Master Joshua	Love & Spiritual Wisdom	Embodying & Existing as Love
3rd	Yellow	Master Serapis Bey	Active Intelligence, Mental Clarity, Manifestation and Discipline	Mastery of Mind & Understanding Energy
4th	Green	Master Paul the Venetian	Creativity, Beauty, Harmony, Balance, Art	Expression of the Creator
5th	Orange	Master Hilarion	Soul Connection & Enhancement, Scientific Developments & Projects	Soul Acceptance and Discovery, Alignment with Creator
6th	Indigo	Master Lanto	Faith & Devotion; Trust & Union with the Creator	Surrendering to the Creator
7th	Violet	Lady Portia	Transformation; Awakening, Cleansing Negativity, Manifesting New Age & Psychic Abilities	Acceptance of Truth on a Conscious Level
8th	Sea-Foam Green	Lady Nada	Spiritual and Energy Cleansing, Releasing and Purifying Being	Cleansing
9th	Blue-Green	Lady Mary	Exploration and Understanding of the Soul	Soul Exploration
10th	Pearlescent	Lady & Master Andromeda	Acceptance	Soul Integration
11th	Pink-Orange	Lady Quan Yin	Embodiment	Soul Integration
12th	Golden	Lady Pallas Athena	Christ Consciousness, Love, Preparation for Solar Level	Soul Integration

Lightning Source UK Ltd.
Milton Keynes UK
UKOW051807030613

211702UK00010B/918/P